The

REEF FISHING BOOK

A Complete Anglers Guide

by Frank Sargeant

Book 1 in the Saltwater Series

Larsen's Outdoor Publishing

ISBN 0-936513-23-3

Library of Congress 95-81614

Published by:

LARSEN'S OUTDOOR PUBLISHING
2640 Elizabeth Place
Lakeland, FL 33813
941/644-3381
FAX 941/644-3288

PRINTED IN THE UNITED STATES OF AMERICA

6 7 8 9 10

ACKNOWLEDGEMENTS

Many thanks to the scientists of the Florida Marine Research Institute in St. Petersburg, Florida for providing information on the growth, age and spawning behaviors of many reef species, and to Chris Koenig at the University of Florida for data on gag grouper. The publication "Memoirs of the Hourglass Cruises", produced by the FMRI lead scientists Lewis Bullock and Gregory Smith in 1991 was particularly helpful. Scientists at Mote Marine Labs in Sarasota were also very cooperative.

Thanks, too, to the many skippers throughout the southeast who shared information, tactics and everything but their loran books with me. Particularly helpful were captains Everett Antrim, Mel Berman, Jim Bradley, Paul Hawkins, Dave Markett, Rob McCue, Joe Penovich, Tom Tamanini, Vance Tice, Robert Trosset, Jerry Williams and James Wisner.

We're also very thankful to Penn Fishing Tackle, which sponsored this book, and to Penn reps Steve Matthews and Gary Walker who provided suggestions on tackle right for all the reef species.

Noted outdoor photographer and writer John Phillips of Fairfield, AL, was kind enough to provide the photos illustrating the red snapper chapter.

Cover Credit: The glass sculpture of the gag grouper was designed by well-known St. Petersburg artist and guide Russ Sirmons, and carved by Rick McCormick. The original is at Billy Moore's Seafoood Restaurant at Tierra Verde Resort in Tierra Verde, FL.

ABOUT THE AUTHOR

Former charterboat skipper Frank Sargeant is one of America's best-known outdoors writers. His work has won more than 50 national awards, and has appeared in most major magazines in the outdoors and boating fields. He is author of eight other fishing books, including the popular Inshore Series on snook, redfish, trout and tarpon, and the Secret Spots Series (see this book's Resource Directory for ordering information). He's a former editor for CBS Publishing Division and senior writer for Walt Disney World Marketing. He has been outdoors editor of the Tampa Tribune for more than a decade, and is a masthead editor for a number of outdoors magazines. He's former president of the Florida Outdoor Writers Association. He holds a masters in English from Ohio University, and has taught writing at the high school and college levels. Sargeant has fished for grouper and snapper for over 30 years. He lives on the Little Manatee River in Ruskin, Florida.

A WORD OF CAUTION

Fishing offshore can be a dangerous business, even for experienced skippers. Anytime you leave protected waters you enter a new world where there is sometimes no second chance to make the right decision. Nothing in this book should be construed as giving the inexperienced boatman encouragement to reach beyond his abilities and experience with the sea. Fishing safely offshore requires large, seaworthy boats, properly maintained. It requires experience in handling a boat in all sea conditions. And it requires a full complement of safety gear and marine electronics. Backup systems are also highly recommended for radio communications and navigation--and for battery power, without which neither of these electronic systems have any use.

It's also wise to carry emergency provisions for three days minimum for the maximum number of passengers your boat can carry, including plenty of fresh water and canned or freeze-dried food. And, of course, no wise skipper ever leaves the docks without checking the weather report--and his bilge pumps. A 15-knot wind--18 mph--causes a Small Craft Advisory or SCA to be issued by the weather service. It's also the limit that sensible anglers set for themselves. In fact, winds over 12 are too much for comfortable fishing if they're blowing onshore, that is, if they have a long fetch before reaching your fishing area.

Grouper and snapper themselves have the potential to do some damage to anglers. Their teeth can inflict painful bites. And the multiple-hook rigs used in trolling can also be dangerous-- especially when they come loose under pressure as the fish nears the boat. Those without the appropriate gear and knowledge should approach live fish with extreme care.

There's also some danger of ciguetera or fish poisoning from eating the flesh of certain reef species. See the chapter on cleaning and cooking for details. In short, there are a number of ways you can get hurt pursuing this sport. Overall, you're a lot safer 20 miles out reeling in reef fish than driving in highway traffic around any urban area these days. But it's always wise to be prepared and be cautious.

CONTENTS

1

THE REEF FISHES: AN INTRODUCTION

The reef fishes include the groupers, snappers and assorted other species, all denizens of the coastal rockpiles, wrecks and coral reefs that decorate offshore waters from the Carolinas to Texas and throughout the Caribbean.

The reef species make up the most colorful assortment of angling targets the sea has to offer. Because these fish depend on coloration matching the brilliant hues of their coral homes as camouflage, they display an unmatched palate of skin tones-- and of confusingly similar species.

For that reason, most species are identified here with their scientific name at the start of each chapter, not because we expect a crusty charterboat skipper to observe that you have just jerked a dandy *Mycteroperca microlepis* aboard, but so that we can be sure that we are all talking about what is in fact the gag grouper, *Mycteroperca microlepis*, and not the black grouper, *Mycteroperca bonaci*.

This book covers the Atlantic species found from Virginia southward to the Florida Keys, and throughout the Gulf of Mexico, and concentrates only on those that are large enough to be of interest to the angler-- hundreds of others not included

Gag grouper, part of a large family of sea basses, are mostly found among rocky outcrops from 20 to 200 feet deep. Gags are probably the most-sought reef species in the Gulf of Mexico.

for lack of space are equally as striking and as fascinating in their life habits.

The groupers belong to a large general category of fishes that scientists call ''serranid'' fishes or sea basses. The grouper most commonly caught by anglers fall into two added divisions based on their body structure, with gags part of the Mycteroperca genus and reds belonging to the Epinephelus genus.

Mycteroperca grouper, which also include black, scamp, yellowfin and yellowmouth, tend to be more streamlined or elongated than the Epinephelus species, more active and mobile, and more likely to attack fairly large live fish as prey.

The more blocky Epinephelus strains are more inclined to depend on camouflage, and are also more inclined to eat cut baits. Species in the genus other than reds include coney, graysby, jewfish, rock hind, red hind, speckled hind, Nassau grouper, warsaw grouper and yellowedge grouper as well as some less common fish. In general, both genuses tend to live in small schools of three to eight fish, with some larger aggregations during spawning. And most grouper are daylight feeders--they sleep in cover at night, with local exceptions in full-moon periods.

Snappers of interest to anglers mostly fall into the Lutjanus genus, which includes cubera, dog, lane, mangrove or gray, mutton and red snapper. These are all fairly flat-bodied fishes compared to the grouper, and all have obvious canine teeth and the inclination to use them, which earns them their family name-- snapper do indeed snap!

Snapper often form large schools that stack up high over an unfished reef, and they're quick to leave the protection of bottom to chase down baitfish passing overhead. The entire genus feeds best after dark, picking up the shift left behind by the grouper.

There are also a number of species that don't quite fit the above categories but that are of high interest to anglers. The yellowtail snapper is not part of the Lutjanus genus--it's really sort of an overgrown aquarium fish--but it's a beautiful animal both on the hook and on the table. And the black sea bass is so common and cooperative that it's included here, as well.

Coloration is a common specifier in determining species of most reef fishes, but be aware that most species are able to change their color to some degree at will. And when hooked or stressed, many will blanch or turn pale, making positive identification more difficult. When most species die their colors become less vivid and sometimes disappear, and fish left in contact with others in an ice box may also turn black on the areas of contact. Learn to identify your fish when it comes over the rail and there's likely to be less confusion when the Marine Patrol arrives to tally up your catch.

While all the reef species were formerly considered "meat" fish, that attitude has moderated a bit in recent years as more anglers become aware that the sea is not an inexhaustible resource, and that no species is invulnerable to over-harvest. This book can help to make you a far better bottom fisherman, but it's up

The red snapper is a popular target in the western Gulf of Mexico as well as along the edge of the continental shelf on Florida's east coast.

to each of us to keep in mind that more knowledge and increased angling skills put more responsibility on the angler for preserving the fisheries.

While reduced bag limits and increased size limits introduced in the last five years have gone a long way toward restoring some hard-fished species, there are more and more recreational anglers each year, and our fish-finding and navigational electronics keep on getting better. With that in mind, smart skippers will avoid fishing out their own numbers and put in place their own conservation programs to assure that their favorite spots remain productive not only for them, but for their children.

2

TACKLING REEF FISH

Tackle for many of the reef species is necessarily stout enough for considerably larger fish. Grouper and the larger snapper are the offensive linemen of the sea, built for power rather than speed, and because they spend much of their lives within 10 feet of their rocky homes, it takes powerful gear to bring them to the top. Tackle otherwise suited for tarpon is about right, though the tarpon may outweigh the grouper by 10 times. This is not to say a grouper is actually stronger than a tarpon, though they might be for that critical distance of 10 feet. But tarpon are not about to go stick their head in a rockpile when hooked.

Some reef fishing pros like fairly long rods, which give them plenty of "sweep" to take up slack when they set the hook. Heavy-butted, two-hand 7- to 8-foot rods with some flex in the tip are the preferred weapons of pros like Capt. Jim Bradley out of Weeki Wachee, Florida, whose favorite is a Penn PC-3821 MH Power Stick (R). On the other side of the state, Capt. Joe Penovich at Port Canaveral also likes a long rod, and chooses a 7' Penn Sabre (R) for pumping up big sow snapper and gags from water up to 200 feet deep.

Short rods or the "stand-up" tackle popular with big-game fishermen have less sweep, but Capt. Robert Trosset of Key West says the shorter sticks do a far better job of lifting fish off the bottom, important when you lock up with a 40-pound black as his clients often do. Trosset likes the 50-pound-class 1760 ARA International II(R) rod for heavy work--it's a 6-foot graphite stick with a short butt and a long foregrip, light in weight and with a sensitive tip but tremendous power in the shaft.

HEADBOAT TACKLE

On most party boats you'll see solid glass rods, chosen for the simple reason that they're almost impossible to break. When tackle is used day after day in bottom fishing, it's truly put to the test. Solid glass survives. It's doubtful you could ever break one on a fish, and some of these rods have even survived being caught in a car door. Solid glass like the venerable Penn Senator(R) series works, and has probably accounted for more bottom fish over the years than all the high-tech sticks combined.

However, there are some major advantages to tubular glass rods like Penn's Slammer (R) and Power Stick(R) models. They're lighter at a given strength, which makes them easier to handle during all-day trips. They're more sensitive so you can better feel the bite, and they're "faster", giving a quicker reaction to a strike, so they improve hook sets. And big game models like the Penn Tuna Stick (R) series include heavy-duty machined aluminum reel seats that will stand the pressure of winching up big fish on heavy line. Cheap reel seats have no place in bottom-fishing due to the loads put on these critical parts.

Tubular fiberglass rods suitable for grouper and snapper are usually built of E-glass, a heavier, high-strength fiber less subject to shattering than standard glass. Some are also built of a composite of graphite and glass, a nice combination which gives you the light weight, stiffness, sensitivity and speed of graphite plus the strength of glass--Penn's Power Graph series contains some nice snapper rods in this construction. Most good ones have the blank all the way through the butt, which gives better strength and sensitivity.

16

All-graphite rods are less popular in bottom-fishing than in other types of angling because their primary benefits, light weight and high tip speed due to stiffness, are of less advantage in plumbing the depths than in casting. They're also far more expensive. But if you can afford it, there's no question that graphites like the International II $^{(R)}$ series are the most comfortable to handle and provide more sensitivity than any other rods.

Whatever material you choose, remember that the stick is only as good as the guides that hold the line in place along its length. For serious bottom-fishing, only the strongest, hardest double-foot guides of silicon carbide, aluminum oxide or chromed stainless or brass are in order. Many quality tubular rods have the guides underwrapped, that is mounted atop a layer of thread, which helps cushion the stick and prevent the metal feet from cutting into the blank under pressure.

Since the maximum line angle on a bottom rod is at the tip, many good rods like Penn's Senator $^{(R)}$ 3240RF have a roller tip-top, greatly reducing friction at this critical spot. Roller guides are not necessary on the rest of the blank because you're not going to have a fish stripping off 200 yards of line at speed, so conventional guides work fine. Of course, you never know when a wahoo is going to grab your grouper bait, so the roller guides on rods like the Special Senator $^{(R)}$ Deluxe series come in handy.

The handle and reel seat are worth a close look in bottom rods. Again, look for strength rather than style. Penn's Nytril $^{(TM)}$ and other dense foam grips have pretty well taken over the market, and they provide a good grip and good durability. One suggestion--avoid rods with extra soft foam, which feels very nice in the store, but which makes it tough to keep the rod aligned properly as it twists against a monster fish. Soft foam soon tears up in rod holders, too. Penn now puts ''Slick Butt'' $^{(TM)}$ graphite grips on many of their bottom/trolling rods, with a density and durability similar to wood, because these stand the wear of the rod holders a lot better.

Penn's famed International Series is more than adequate for taking on even the giants of the reef. The lever drag allows a quick reduction of tension if a wahoo or kingfish grabs your grouper bait--otherwise, the brute strength of these reels does the job with the drag locked down tight to winch big grouper away from their rocky homes.

Wood grips are also durable. The foregrip, though, should be lengthy and made of medium foam, because here's where you apply the work with your hands. Round grips seem to work best for most people--triangles and other shapes tend to bother the hands if you have a really heavy day of grouper pulling. (These are problems we all should have!)

The butt cap that works best for most anglers is a straight plastic job. While "belly saver" butts with some sort of rubber or cork bumper on them definitely make it less likely you'll wind up with a black-and-blue groin (ouch!) these devices make it impossible to put the rod into a conventional upright trolling rod holder. They can be stored horizontally under the gunnels, of course, but most who have tried them eventually take them off.

(A tip: hollow out a foam-rubber playball to fit the butt of your favorite rods. Attach it to the rod when you're ready to fish, keep it in your pocket between spots.)

Gimble-style or slotted metal rod butts are useful if you troll a lot because they fit the pegs in many rod holders and keep the rod straight. However, these slotted butts are murder on the gut if you ever grab one attached to a heavy fish and don't have a fighting belt in place. If you go for the slotted butts, consider a stand-up belt a part of the price. Sampo makes a neat all-day gimbal that fits over your own belt--it's called the "Hookup", and goes for about 12 bucks. The snap-on plastic jobs are quick and easy, too--PlayAction makes a good one for about $50, but you have to buy them within the belly-size range of your crew--difficult if you have both thin kids and large-bellied beer-drinkers aboard. The standard Velcro web belts start at around $15. You should have one type or the other aboard at all times.

REELS

Most anglers choose revolving spool reels that can hold 200 to 350 yards of 50-pound-test mono--generally, reels designated between 2/0 and 4/0. You don't need big line capacity, but you do need fairly stout line for serious bottom fishing, and the stout gears to back it up. Basic needs are great frame and gear strength, rather than castability or an exceptionally smooth drag--as the best bottom-diggers know, if the drag slips, you're probably going to lose the fish when it comes to dredging up big grouper.

The venerable Penn Senator 113H [R] probably accounts for 80 percent of the reels used for bottom fishing, with good reason. These work-horses are known for amazing strength and durability as well as a price that won't break the budget. The 113H has a chrome-plated bronze spool that's one of the strongest in the industry, bronze alloy main gears with a fast 3.25:1 ratio, stainless pinion gears and oversized power-handles that take some of the work out of cranking up a 20-pounder. Ball bearings promise smooth operation and a long life. Weight is 34 ounces, no light weight, but not enough to wear you out fighting the tackle instead of the fish.

If you like a little more cranking power, the 113 might be the ticket. (These have black side-plates rather than the red of the H-Senator series.) The standard Senator $^{(R)}$ has a winch-like 2:1 gear ratio, which makes it possible to crank even the toughest fish away from cover. It has bushings rather than ball bearings, but it's also less expensive than the H models.

If you want a more economical reel that's just as tough as the Senator $^{(R)}$, take a look at the Penn Long Beach $^{(R)}$ bottom fishing series. The Model 66, for example, holds 275 yards of 50-pound test, weighs in at just 26 ounces, and features a stainless steel spool. The retrieve ratio is a good compromise of speed and power at 2.5:1. Or if you're more into fishing jigs, you might like the Jigmaster $^{(R)}$ series, a lightweight reels that can handle line up to 30 pound test and offers retrieve rates of 4:1 or 5:1; these are nice dual-personality reels that would work well for king mackerel as well as the bottom species. The new 555GS offers a very quick 5.3:1 ratio for even faster retrieves.

If you prefer a level-wind reel, the GTi series provides smooth spooling in sizes up to 5/0--the 345 GTi holds 375 yards of 50 pound test, yet weighs in at just 34 ounces thanks to a corrosion-proof, lightweight all-graphite frame.

For those who fish long and hard for record fish, like Capt. Robert Trosset, the added cost of the gold-adonized International$^{(R)}$ Series lever-drag reels is worth the money. Trosset uses a 30-Wide International$^{(R)}$ loaded with 50-pound-test mono for most of his grouper and red-snapper fishing, and should a blackfin tuna or a white marlin happen along, he's ready.

ELECTRIC REELS

Adding electric power to a reel is expensive and takes some extra wiring, but these power-winders take a lot of the work out of fishing water deeper than 200 feet. Elec-Tra-Mate is the

Graphite framed reels like the 5000 GCS cut weight while still delivering lots of strength. Reels in this class are ideal for mangrove and mutton snapper fishing.

best-known maker--their 440-XP is designed for the Penn 113H series, and is the one most grouper/snapper fishermen want. This model runs around $250, without the reel. Winders for 6/0 and 9/0 Penn reels are also available. Electric reels are not sporty, but they're the only practical way to fish really deep water.

LIGHT TACKLE

Can you catch big grouper and sow snapper on light tackle?

Yes, and you can hunt grizzly bears with a bow and arrow, too, but I wouldn't advise it unless you have a .375 magnum to back up the sharp stick. There's a place for light tackle entertainment in bottom fishing, though. Particularly when the fish are shallow and responding to chum, it's possible to play with them on light gear, and some folks get absolutely addicted to this challenge, even though they sometimes come home without much in the box. If you don't mind fairly frequent "Palm Beach releases", there's no reason not to have a go at it.

Some of the better tackle for this include reels like Penn's 320 GTi, a corrosion proof graphite-framed model that scales just 19.5 ounces and is designed for 20-pound-test mono. This level wind reel with sealed stainless ball bearings is a nice rig for casting. Buckled up with a medium duty rod like the Penn Slammer ® SLC-2661AX, this rig has adequate power to handle the biggest mangrove snapper as well as some very substantial gags, but enough action for casting jigs and live baits.

Some snapper pros like Capt. Robert Trosset also like medium spinning gear for yellowtails and muttons. Trosset recommends a Penn 6500SS spinner loaded with 15-pound-test on a 7-foot rod like the new Spinfisher® Big Game SBG 6770 or a Power Stick® 4821M. To live bait for red snapper, he moves up to a Penn 8500SS spinner with 30-pound-test and a stouter rod like the Slammer ® 7722. It's a good rod for deep-jigging with up to 3-ounce heads. All the SS reels have a stainless main shaft extending from the spool through the reel housing. Bronze bushings at the back of the housing provide support and maintain perfect alignment.

Even the baitcasters so popular with fresh water bass anglers have a place in light tackle reef fishing, if you don't overline them. While largemouth bass anglers routinely load these reels up with 30-pound-test and lock down the drag to winch bass from heavy cover, try that trick on a 20-pound red snapper and you may have problems. However, in areas where only 'tails or mangrove snapper are present, a revolving spool reel like the venerable Penn 940 Levelmatic ® loaded with 15-pound-test can provide lots of sport plus easy casting. With a weight of just 11.5 ounces and an anodized gold finish to match the big brother International® Series, these reels are durable and strong. A good matchup rod is the Penn Power Graph™ PG 5971, a graphite composite that can handle lines to 25-pound-test.

Some snapper fishermen prefer heavy-duty spinning reels like the 9500 SS for jigging deep reefs with artificials. Since there's no spool over-run with spinning gear, the drop to bottom is made simple.

LINES

Monofilament is the standard, hard to beat for economy and dependability. Any well-known brand will do the job, and most anglers prefer 40- to 50-pound test for all-around reef action on gags, red grouper and large red snapper. Anglers after bigger fish in deeper water might opt for 80-pound mono, while those fishing shallower water for fish under 10 pounds might choose 30-pound test. Whatever you use, be sure to check the last 20 feet regularly during a day of fishing. The line often gets pulled over reefs and wrecks, causing tiny cuts that will give way when a big fish is hooked.

Dacron line, long a favorite for trollers, also works well for bottom fishing. The line has very little stretch, so provides a more solid strike and more power to pull fish away from the bottom.

However, it is highly visible and somewhat buoyant, both negatives in reef bumping. Anglers who use Dacron usually run about 20 feet of heavy mono as a leader.

Some anglers have switched to the new Spectra braided lines with good results. Their cable-like absence of stretch and their great strength-to-diameter ratio, are both pluses in bottom fishing. You get better hook sets, and you also get a lot better pull against the first panicked run back toward the rocks.

The negatives of braids are their great cost--three to five times that of mono--and their somewhat suspect knot-strength. Most slip or cut into themselves, dropping their strength considerably. Of course, you can go up in pound-test to compensate. It's worth trying a spool to see if you like it. Berkley's new Fire Line, which fuses the line after braiding, seems to have better knot-strength than some, and is exceptionally easy to cast.

Wire line, which allows deep trolling without a downrigger or planer, comes in monel or stainless, and from 60-to 200-pound test. With wire, though, you're more interested in the weight per foot than the breaking strength. Typical monel 60-pound-test requires 425 feet to weigh a pound, while monel 110-pound-test takes only 200 feet to the pound. Obviously, the heavier stuff gets deep faster, but its larger diameter requires a bigger reel. In general, you need a 6/0 to fish 60-pound, a 9/0 for 95-pound-test and a 12/0 for 110-pound-test. Narrow-spool reels like the Penn Mariner(R) 49L work best for controlling the wire. It's also best to use a rod with a swivel tip and a roller. Other types of tips will be quickly grooved by the wire, but the combination of the swivel and roller keeps the wire centered on the roller for better longevity.

HOOKS

Bottom-fishing hooks have to be stout to stand the pressure of locked-down drags on heavy gear. Most gag, red grouper and red snapper anglers prefer heavy wire stock, 5/0 to 8/0, with

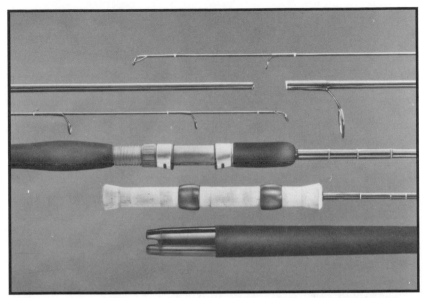

Penn Power Graph rods are a fiberglass/graphite combination that produces a rod with the strength of fiberglass and the light weight and sensitivity of graphite. They're a good choice for shallow reefs, and for light biters like snapper.

the O'Shaughnessy style C46 3407 and the Mustad 3407 among the favorites. Lighter hooks will simply open up when put under pressure on 40- to 60-pound-test line, so there's no point in going light to keep the baits lively, as many inshore anglers do.

One thing you might do with these hooks is to reduce the barb slightly with a file, honing it down to about half normal size. This results in much quicker sinking of the hook, and can make a difference in your catch, particularly in deep water where there's a lot of line stretch and much of your striking force is not translated to the hook.

Circle hooks, used by offshore longliners, are good for deep water where the bite is not readily transmitted to the rod, and for beginning anglers who have a hard time knowing when to strike. The hooks look as if they couldn't catch anything, since they are almost literally complete circles, but they manage to burrow their point into fish jaws with amazing consistency. And once the point goes home, the barb always follows due to the design of the hook. You never pull one free once it's set. For those of the "now who's the jerk" school--they don't believe in setting the hook, but rather in letting the fish hook itself while the angler simply starts reeling--the circle hook is a major advantage. Note that these hook sizes are much different from conventional hooks--an 11/0 or 12/0 is not too big for grouper and large red snapper, while in conventional hooks most anglers don't use anything larger than a 9/0.

LEAD

Every bottom fisherman needs roughly his own weight in leads stowed aboard. Everything from 2 ounces to 8 ounces will be useful in water up to 100 feet deep at times, and in deeper water it sometimes pays to carry some true blackjacks, weights approaching a full 16 ounces. Of course, on a calm day with no tide running, a 1/4 ounce lead will hit bottom in 100 feet of water. But on the typical day offshore, you'll be fighting both wind and tide, and the more of each, the more lead you need to plummet your bait quickly and accurately to the bottom.

Remember, a strong current can "blow" your lead and bait as much as 30 feet off the vertical in a 100-foot drop, and that's enough to move it completely out of the strike zone for fish hugged in tight on the rock showing on your screen. If you show lots of fish but aren't getting any hookups and there's strong current running, it often pays to double the weight on your rigs, which will send the bait on a rocket-sled ride straight down to the fish.

Best weights? The cheapest you can get, because you'll lose plenty. Most anglers slide the weight directly on the running line above a single large barrel swivel--it's a quick, effective rig, and it allows the fish to run off with the bait without dragging the sinker because the line runs free through the hole in the lead.

Some anglers are concerned about the friction of the weight working against the line, and block the lead in place with swivels on either end of a 6-inch length of 125-pound-test mono. This can save you some fish if you use mono lighter than 50-pound-test as your running line.

With either rigging, the bait dangles 2 to 5 feet below the lead, with the leader 50-pound-test mono in clear water, 80-pound in dingy or deeper water. If you're a glutton for punishment, put one hook on the bottom of the rig, another about 4 feet up the line on an 18" dropper and try for a double-header. You're in trouble if a pair of 20-pound gags takes hold, though.

DOWNRIGGERS

Downriggers can make almost any reef angler more successful because they put the bait or lure down where the grouper and snapper live, right next to the bottom. It's very tough to maintain consistent depth while trolling without a rigger, but experienced 'rigger anglers can estimate to within a foot exactly how deep their rig is running at a given speed. It provides a huge advantage. Penn's Fathom-Master $^{(R)}$ models offer gear-driven cable meters that measure exactly how far down the weight has been lowered, making it easy to control presentations at any depth up to 200 feet. The Electric Fathom-Master $^{(R)}$ 800 includes a powerful 12-volt motor to retrieve the rigger ball at up to 135 feet per minute, while the Fathom-Master $^{(R)}$ 600 is an economical manual model. Both feature corrosion-proof, glass-reinforced polycarbonate spool, base and frame, anodized aluminum booms in 2-foot or 4-foot lengths and 135-pound-test stainless steel cable.

TACKLE MAINTENANCE

Whatever tackle you use, it will last a lot longer and give fewer problems if you expose it to salt as little as possible. Though many anglers like to stick their gear in the trolling holders for the run offshore, on windy or rough days, that location usually results in a briny bath for the gear. It's much better to store the tackle under the gunnels or in the cabin until you're ready to fish, and to put it back in these locations for the run home.

And, when you get to the docks, the best reel treatment is a plunge into a 5-gallon bucket full of clean fresh water. Some anglers add a bit of dish soap, others avoid it because the soap washes out gear grease and bearing oil. Spray off the reel with fresh water, but don't use a hard, driving spray or you risk pushing salt and sand into the reel's innards! Just wash the salt off the exterior surfaces, and don't forget to rinse the guides thoroughly. Be religious about the freshwater wash, lube your reels regularly and your tackle will last forever.

Many anglers also like to finish off the cleanup operations with a shot of spray oil to all external surfaces. The best product I've found for this is Corrosion-X. It's a light lubricant that seems to wash away the green crud that often starts around screws and small parts. And it doesn't leave a film when it dries, as some similar products do. Spray it on, wipe off the excess and you're good to go. It's available at most marine dealers. (The stuff is also great for electrical connections, and does not harm components of most electronics--some repair shops actually submerge corroded depthfinders in a bucket of the stuff, leave them in there 24 hours, and when they come out they work!)

Finally, remember to back off the drags on all reels between trips. This allows drag washers to dry more thoroughly and takes tension off any springs and cupped washers. The result is a smoother, longer-lasting drag system.

3

LOCATION, LOCATION, LOCATION

Before you can catch 'em, you've got to find 'em, and in grouper and snapper fishing, you soon discover that there are a whole lot of places where they ain't. In bottom fishing, as in real estate, the three secrets of success are location, location and location.

FINDING THE RIGHT ZIP CODE

General fish location, getting in the neighborhood, is easy. Finding the buildings where the big fish hang out is hard. Everybody will give you neighborhood numbers, and the nice thing about this is that rocks travel in schools--where there's one, there are usually a whole lot more, so if you get in the area of a community number--which you can get from local skippers, fishing magazines, fishing reports in newspapers and commercial charts and dive books--and then begin to troll methodically, you'll soon have more good numbers than you can fish in a day.

Of course, it does no good to visit Miami when everybody has gone to New Orleans for the Mardi Gras, so you must time your fishing in a given zone to the fish migrations. Charterboat skippers will often admit to how far out or how deep they're fishing, even though they won't share any numbers with you. So get this information first--you can expect action inshore when water temperatures are between 68 and 80, prime weather for most species of grouper and snapper. If it's either hotter or colder, the fish are likely farther offshore where depth provides insulation against the extremes. Thus, along the Florida Gulf Coast, spring fishing may be in water as shallow as 8 feet, while by August the action will be at 45 to 80 feet as much as 50 miles offshore in the northeastern Gulf. Expert skippers say they see some fish on the inshore rocks even in the hottest weather, but it's very difficult to get them to bite. Best strategy is to go where the fish want to cooperate, and that means a long ride.

FIND THE PATTERN

The best search pattern is "grid" trolling, the same sort of pattern the Coast Guard uses in search and rescue to make sure they adequately cover the water.

Troll a mile north, then maybe a tenth west, then a mile south, then a tenth west again, then a mile north, and so on until you catch fish or at least mark a good show on the sonar.

And always keep your eyes open for what the sea is willing to give you free. If you spot turtles popping up for air, it's a sign of live bottom below. And often, so are baitfish splashing on top, birds flying or sitting on the water, and porpoises rolling in open sea. In clear water, you may be able to actually see reef areas at depths up to 40 feet in the Gulf and as much as 80 feet in the Atlantic--they show as darker green or deep blue blotches in the lighter shades of sand bottom surrounding them.

JUG IT

One key piece of gear in this process is a good marker jug, usually a gallon plastic jug with light nylon cord wrapped around it to a length at least 15 feet longer than the deepest water you'll fish. Yellow milk jugs are a favorite--they're much easier to see than white or clear jugs, especially when the whitecaps are rolling. Anchor is a 1-pound or heavier weight--don't use less weight or wind and current will blow it off your spot.

The ability to mark a good location once you find it is critical to successful reef fishing. Marker floats help to fix position in the otherwise featureless offshore waters.

When a likely spot shows on the screen, have a crewman heave this aft immediately. The weight causes the cord to unroll and anchor the jug directly over the structure. Use a couple of rubber bands to limit the amount of line that unrolls to just enough to hit bottom. Otherwise you have to wind it all up when you pick up the jug. A handy alternative is the Suremark anchoring buoy, which has a small built-in reel right in the float, plus a flag that projects several feet above the surface. It keeps the line right where you want it, never snarled, and it's a neat package. It's about $50 from Suremark Distributors, 1252 Boyd Avenue, Sarasota, FL 34237, (813) 365-1298.

Once the marker is down, you return to troll in concentric circles around the jug, keeping an eye on the screen for the mother lode. Many times, you pass over only a small corner of the main rock, and a few circles will reveal the real hotspot. Don't keep trolling once you've got the spot zeroed, though--excessive motor noise may put the fish down, particularly in water less than 50 feet deep. When you're ready to anchor, look at the jug to get an idea how the "set" or current will work on the boat and drop the hook accordingly. (Most smart anglers pull

This float includes a flag that juts well above the waves, making it easy to see. A built-in reel stores the line.

in the jug before they start fishing--otherwise, a hooked fish will surely tangle with the line.)

Record each spot where you get bit or where you get an interesting show on the screen, and try these numbers each time you're in the area. It takes time and patience, but it works consistently, and it's money in the bank--after you secure 50 or 100 spots, they're yours, and you don't have to search for new spots if you don't overfish them.

(One strange anomally occurs in the shallow waters of the Gulf of Mexico during many hurricane seasons. Because a major storm can move sand around in depths out to 40 feet and more, grouper anglers often find that their favorite reefs have completely disappeared after a big storm, and brand new rockpiles and breaks have magically appeared where there were none before. It's heck on updating your GPS or loran numbers, but when you find one of these new rocks it's usually red hot for a few weeks.)

UNDERWATER CITIES

Picture an underwater reef or rockpile like a highrise city. If you drop your bait on Broadway, nobody who lives on Fifth Avenue is going to be able to see it because of the intervening buildings. It's the same on a tall reef or break. Unless the fish are up high above the cover--as they sometimes are when they're in a feeding mood--the ones on the south side of the rock won't see your bait if it falls on the north side, even if the distance between the right spot and the wrong one is only 10 feet.

How do you know if your bait falls in the right spot? You get a bite from one of your target species. Grouper are not all that selective if they haven't been alerted by a noisy approach and haven't been fished hard. If a fresh sardine or pinfish lands in front of their nose, 90 percent of the time they're going to grab it, especially on the first couple of drops.

THE RED ZONE

Snapper are a little more cautious, but they're also quick to bite if you deliver a tasty live bait and haven't made them nervous on the approach. If you don't get that near immediate bite, you can bet that you're on the wrong street. Divers note that grouper and snapper often concentrate in a piece of rock only 15 feet wide, along a reef that's several hundred feet long. You have to land near that "red zone" to get the bite.

One approach is fan-casting, which delivers the bait over a wide area, but also results in lots more snags than a vertical drop and also makes it hard to land a big fish, particularly from the "off" side of a rock, the side away from the boat.

Better, but more labor-intensive, is to keep moving the boat until you get the spot exactly right for a vertical drop into the end zone. It sometimes requires considerable patience to get to the spot you need to be on--relocating a half-dozen times on a single anchor point is not uncommon for a good skipper scoping out a new spot.

You do this with the tactics described in the next chapter on anchoring--basically, it's a matter of letting out a few feet of line at a time, and then exploring to the right and left of that zone by turning the wheel and letting the lower unit act as a rudder to scoot the boat sideways in the tideflow. This is very effective when winds are moderate and in the same direction as the tide, less so in stronger winds or beam winds. In any case the task is to probe all the spots on the reef for that one honeyhole, the intersection of Broadway and Fifth, where all the studs hang out. (One tip: when you hook a fish, note which way it goes on the first run. If it's a gag, it will almost always run for the biggest ledge around, and that's probably where the mother lode of fish is located. Cast that way, or move the boat in that direction, and you're likely to connect with more fish.)

The similarity with downtown extends to the way the reef runs, too. If there's a bakery on Fifth Avenue and the wind is blowing down that street, everybody downwind of the bake shop is going to get hungry for doughnuts anytime the ovens are working. But the people over one street on Broadway won't get a whiff, and so won't go around the corner to get their lemon-filled and chocolate-coated.

Reefs in most areas are like streets, narrow and long instead of circular or squared. If you get on the uptide end of a reef and put down your bait--or even better a chum pot and then your bait--everybody downstream is going to get the scent and come over for a snack. So it makes sense to target the up-current end of a reef first, and then ease down on the anchor line until you work the area out. You can figure all this out by keeping a sharp eye on the depthfinder as you circle your number or a show of fish, and using jugs to line out the area. For this reason, it makes good sense to keep at least two jugs at ready--an extra fixed reference point can make all the difference between coming home with a limit and coming home with an empty box.

WHEN TO GO

It's also possible to be at just the right address at just the wrong time--you don't see many people in restaurants at 3 in the afternoon, but go back at 7 p.m. and they're jammed. The

Bouncing a tipped jig on bottom is a good way to locate action once you're in the right zip code. Lure manufacturer Steve Marusak, of Cotee Jigs, shows he knows how to use 'em as well as design 'em.

same is true of grouper and snapper--they're not in a feeding mood all the time. Some old salts anchor up where they see a big show of fish on the depthfinder and stay there for an hour or so, even though there's no bite, on the theory that all those fish sooner or later will get ready to eat. It takes a different mental set from the run-and-gun approach which suggests that 10 minutes is long enough on any spot that's not producing, but it works, too. In general, extreme tide-flows don't produce the best fishing--apparently the fish keep tucked into the structure so they don't have to fight the current. But the back side of a strong flow, when the current moderates, may produce gangbuster action.

As to the right time of the month to go fishing--it's any time you have a day off. Great catches are made every day of the month. However, there does seem to be something to the idea that the week leading up to the full moon and new moon are most productive, maybe because stronger currents then move the bait around and make the fish more active. And most long-time bottom fishermen are convinced that the major periods listed in the Knight's Solunar tables consistently produce a good bite.

A lot of anglers get disappointed on their first four or five trips offshore when they come back with zip, and give it up on the theory that there are not enough grouper or snapper left in the coastal waters to bother with. Don't believe it. In most areas, there are plenty of fish, but you have to put in the time to find their homes. It takes persistence, a methodical approach and the confidence that you'll eventually succeed--and you will, if you stick to it.

A final word: once you find the right address, don't pull out all the residents at once. Prime fishing on a set of numbers lasts only a couple of visits, and many grouper and snapper pros try to rotate their spots so that they never hit the same location more than once every 30 to 60 days. That means you have to have a lot of spots--you should be on the lookout anytime the boat is underway--but that you can depend on each to produce each time you visit.

4

GAG GROUPER

Mycteroperca microlepsis, the gag grouper, is the most popular of all the reef species in the eastern Gulf of Mexico. Gags are fishing favorites because they're big and tough and nasty--and because they taste great. They're found in the Atlantic from Massachusetts (not many) to Florida (lots), and throughout the Gulf of Mexico and in the Caribbean to Brazil.

Big gags, commonly called "black" grouper in some localities, freight-train a live bait and can pull the strongest angler to his knees on the initial power-run toward their rocky home. Gags are charcoal gray with mottling that looks almost like kiss marks on their sides. They do get big--the IGFA record is 80 pounds, 6 ounces, caught off Destin. That giant is truly outsized, though: anything over 25 pounds is a real trophy, and the average gag brought to the docks goes 7 to 9 pounds.

WHERE TO FIND THEM

The vast majority of both the recreational and commercial catch--up to 9 million pounds a year--come from the northeastern Gulf, roughly north of Tampa Bay and around the curve of Florida to the Alabama line.

Though gags are most often caught today in water deeper than 20 feet, historically they were found over rock piles in water as shallow as five feet. The change is not due to changed habits

Gags are the most abundant grouper in the northeastern Gulf. They're less numerous along the Atlantic shelf, but reach larger average sizes.

but rather to the fishing pressure and poorer inshore water quality. In some areas good catches of very respectable fish can still be had periodically over water only 10 feet deep--on topwater plugs!

At the other end of the scale, gags are found out to 500-foot depths. The largest fish, over 25 pounds, most often come from water deeper than 100 feet, maybe because all the big ones are picked off inshore before they can reach their maximum. Gags are strongly attracted to major reefs and big ledges, and aren't often found on the smaller structures and reliefs that attract other reef fish.

The prime gag grouper grounds are from Anclote Key north to the Suwannee River, where the entire bottom of the gulf is composed of limerock. In many areas this bedrock is covered with a thin layer of sand and there are no fish, but anywhere it peeks through, gags and other bottom species gather. Thus, there's good fishing from water as little as 8 feet deep right on out to the Middle Grounds. This is an area of patch reefs in water 100 to 150 feet deep, roughly due south of Cape San Blas and due west of Weeki Wachee. December through April, the area is home to monster spawners in the 20- to 40-pound class.

Some of the best gag waters in the "Big Bend" area, the curve of Florida where the peninsula meets the panhandle, are found in 30 to 40 foot depths in winter, and the water is generally so clear that it's possible for a trained eye to pick out the reefs by watching through Polarized glasses. The reef areas look dark green, as opposed to the pale green of sand bottom. Good fall and spring fishing begins in as little as 15 feet of water in the eastern portions of this area, the so-called "short rocks", while farther west the best structure shows up farther out. November though March is prime time, though spells of freezing weather may put the fish off their feed for up to a week at a time. Prime water temperature seems to be 65 to 72 degrees--colder or hotter and the bite slows down.

To find big fish in this area, though, it's more common to run farther out, 50 to 70 feet, where your depthfinder takes the place of your eyes. This is particularly true in summer, when few decent fish are found inshore.

Farther west, the best gag areas are in water deeper than 100 feet, many miles from land. The 132-foot break, a noted producer, is 32 miles south of Mexico Beach, Florida, while the

When they're in water less than 40 feet deep, gags make a good target for heavy spinning tackle. Both live baits and jigs do the job when worked around sharp relief rockpiles and ledges.

195-foot break is at 35 miles. Some of the biggest fish, including the all-tackle world record gag caught aboard Capt. Kelly Windes' charterboat Sunrise out of Destin by angler Bill Smith come from 200 to 250-foot depths here. Interestingly, a few expert charterboat captains also locate lots of keeper gags inside the major bays here on shallow-water wrecks. St. Andrews, Choctawhatchee and Pensacola bays all have viable fisheries.

Gags are not as abundant between Clearwater and Venice, except on isolated wrecks and on reefs that are far offshore. The inshore bottom has few prominent reefs, and so does not attract a lot of gags, though its "Swiss cheese" structure holds plenty of red grouper. The ship channels of Tampa Bay produce very good fishing at times, as do the rocks around the new Skyway

Bridge, and the artificial reefs created with the rubble of the old bridge.

At Boca Grand Pass, entrance to Charlotte Harbor, the deep, rocky holes that lure tarpon in summer pull in lots of nice gags in March and April. The 45- and 72-foot drops on the north side of the pass are both noted for producing nice gags, with deep-jigging with a 2- to 4-ounce tipped bucktail a favored tactic.

Gags are abundant between Naples and Marco, where a series of long reefs run off to the northwest. Some of these ridges start in only 20 feet of water, but the bigger fish are usually taken in deeper areas. Anglers who don't have numbers in this area simply troll GPS headings northwest and southeast, often working in and out of the fish as the reef rises from the sand bottom, then sinks back into it.

And gags also invade the passes and deep rivers of the Everglades and 10,000 Islands area. Many of these outflows have more than 10 feet of water and rocky bottoms, and they frequently hold keeper-sized gags. A big fish in this country is 10 pounds, but when you consider that you can catch them on baitcasters here, they become formidable adversaries. Jigs tipped with cut fish do well, as do live shrimp or baitfish bumped along bottom with the tide. (Don't be surprised if your grouper bait is grabbed by a snook or a tarpon.)

On the east coast of Florida, gags are commonly called ''gray'' grouper. Check out the 14-mile-long sub channel dredged out of the St. Mary's river near Fernandina Beach. The steep walls of this cut always hold bait and frequently produce nice gags. Off the St. Johns River mouth near Jacksonville gags are found from 50 foot-depths on out. Best action is along the drops at the edge of the continental shelf, usually in fall and spring. The fish may be between 10 and 20 miles out during these prime times. In colder and hotter months, they're farther out, up to 60 miles off--farther than most care to run to get them.

Farther south along Florida's east coast, there's good groupering on the 21-Fathom Drop between Daytona and Canaveral. Captain Joe Penovich at Canaveral reports that gag action turns on in December and remains hot through March at depths of 80 to 180 feet. The fish run big here, with the average catch 16 to 18 pounds. Live spot is the favored local bait.

Gags are also numerous at 27-Fathom Ridge off Ft. Pierce, and at The Steeples, a long chain of jagged topography found at around 60 fathoms. Off Jupiter Inlet the 20-fathom curve has a very obvious break that's a favorite not only for gags but also true black grouper.

There's a "bite" of gags on the offshore reefs around the Keys January to March, which may be a spawning aggregation. They're not all that common there at other times.

GRASS GROUPER

Gags are also known as "grass grouper" during their early years, because juveniles up to about 12 inches use the deeper grass flats as their natural habitat. It's very common to catch a dozen of these gray-green mottled grouper while drifting the deep grass anywhere between Anclote Key, just north of Clearwater, Florida, and the Big Bend area--all a broad, clear grass flat that extends up to 10 miles offshore. In fact, these little gags used to be considered "sandwich" grouper before the size limits made their harvest illegal, and that take of juveniles was a major reason that the fishery was on the downslide until the rules went into place. Scientists pulling trawls have found that in prime habitat, the grass flats may support up to 200 juvenile gags per acre, making it clear that this habitat is critical for maintaining the offshore reef fishery.

Young gags feed mostly on shrimp and small fish and are easy to catch on shrimp-like jigs bounced on bottom. But since they can't be harvested it's best to avoid catching them and possibly causing release mortality. The abundance of this excellent

42

The battle is over when a gag comes to the top. For the first 15 to 20 feet above bottom, though, they're one of the strongest of all fish.

habitat for young fish may be the reason that the prime fishery for adult gags is found off this area, in the northeastern Gulf.

SEASONAL MOVEMENTS

Though many bottom-diggers believe gags head offshore when the water gets cold, some divers say that they stay put. If so, it's likely that the fish feed less in cold water, so are harder to catch inshore during those mornings when there's frost on the windshield. Grouper in deeper water would be less affected by the temperature change, so would continue to bite, giving rise to the migration theory. (On the other hand, maybe they really do move--in any case, the bite is sure a lot better when the water warms a bit in spring. Off the west-central coast of Florida, the action usually begins by Easter, but can be slow earlier if the weather is cool.)

Gags are among the most active of groupers, and don't stay glued to the reef like some species--that's why you'll occasionally troll up a big one and then go back to search in vain for his rockpile and his buddies. Gags are also not afraid to rise to the top on occasion, a fact that savvy guides like Captain Jim Bradley of Weeki Wachee, Florida, use to advantage when they chum gags to the surface with live sardines.

"Grass grouper" are juvenile gags, found most often over deep grass flats. They're not legal for harvest due to the minimum 20-inch size limit.

Gags are somewhat more streamlined than red grouper, and don't weigh as much at a given length. A 20-inch legal fish weighs 4 to 5 pounds and is about 3 years old. A 24-incher is likely to weigh around 8 to 10 pounds at age 4, while a 28-incher goes between 12 and 15 pounds at age 5 or 6. A yard-long fish, should you ever be so lucky to see one, may scale between 22 and 28 pounds and be about 10 years old, while fish over 30 pounds may exceed 40 inches and be 15 to 20 years old.

There are plans in progress to close the season January through March, to protect the large copper belly males on the deep reefs and also to cut the overall harvest inshore. Since the males are the most aggressive and quickest to bite when the spawn is on, the shutdown could help improve stocks. A recent study from the Gulf of Mexico Fishery Management Council found that gag numbers have held steady since the 20-inch minimum size was put in place. That's the good news. The bad news is that the sex ratio went from 6:1 female in the late 1970's to 34:1 female by the early 1990's.

GROUPER CONSERVATION

Like many grouper, gags are what biologists call "protogynous hermaphrodites, which means they begin life as females, with a major portion turning to males as they grow older. Most females reach sexual maturity at 5 to 7 years. The sex change apparently occurs in those that reach age 9 or older, which accounts for the giant "copper belly" males, 40 to 60 pounds, found on the deep reefs of the Gulf during spawning aggregations.

While inshore grouper stocks are doing well thanks to the elimination of longline fishing in Florida waters and tight size and bag limits, offshore where the parent fish live there may be trouble brewing. According to biologist Chris Koenig of Florida State University, the adult stocks of gags on the deep reefs are being drastically overfished, to the point that large males or "copperbellies" are almost extinct. Reportedly only about 2 percent of adult gags survive to become spawning males.

It's unknown how many spawners have to survive to replenish the inshore grass flats where the young fish grow up, but there's obviously a limit and Koenig and other scientists believe we are at it--or beyond.

Koenig says many fish caught at 40 to 200 meters don't survive the trip to the surface due to the pressure changes. While bottom fish caught in shallow water nearly all survive if their bladder is deflated before release, he says up to 95 percent of fish caught from the deeper areas die. He says a closure from January through June would protect all three primary reef species during the spawn when they are most vulnerable. Gags, in particular, are heavily harvested because they congregate in large groups during the spawn, and because they aggressively bite baited hooks at this time. The big males, rare to begin with, have been observed to be the first to bite a baited hook that lands among the spawners.

Gag populations are currently doing well--except for the largest male fish found in the deep gulf, where scientists say over-harvest is reducing spawning capacity. Conservation-wise anglers release all fish not wanted for the table both to preserve good local fishing spots and for the future success of the species.

GAG RESEARCH

A 10-pound gag grouper is not your typical aquarium pet, but then Carole Neidig doesn't operate your typical aquarium. The senior biologist with Mote Marine Labs in Sarasota oversees grouper kept in 20-foot-wide lab tanks. The long-term study of the species' reproductive biology may someday influence how the fishery is regulated.

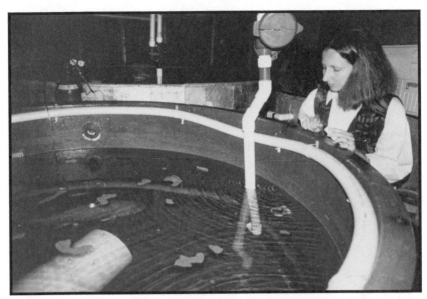

Carol Neidig, senior biologist with Mote Marine Labs in Sarasota oversees grouper kept in 20-foot-wide lab tanks. The long-term study of the species' reproductive biology may someday influence how the fishery is regulated.

Her assessment of grouper personalities? "They're pigs," she vows. "They eat just about every time you offer them food and they'll eat up to 20 percent of their body weight in a day. They eat so much they have to spit it out."

One of the fish got so enthusiastic at the hand-feeding that it became risky to get close to the tank.

"He bit eight people. We took pictures of the wounded hands and hung them on the tank, but he just kept getting more people," said Neidig. "Sometimes he jumped out of the water to grab someone's hand."

They should be so hungry when you drop a hooked pinfish in front of them.

Neidig said that the captive fish gained weight at an incredible rate of 20 to 50 percent per year, raising the possibility that the

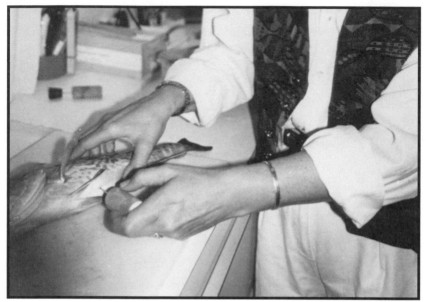

Neidig shows the correct method of deflating a grouper so that it can be released successfully in deep water. Most fish that are deflated survive repeated captures, even in water 100 feet deep.

species might be a good bet for aquaculture. Farmed grouper would reduce the pressure on wild stocks, as well as increasing the availability of this very valuable seafood.

The Mote study, funded by the National Marine Fisheries Service, is a cooperative effort with Dr. Craig Sullivan of North Carolina State University to learn the conditions that lead to grouper spawning, the internal changes that trigger the spawn, and the conditions that yield sex change in gags and other groupers.

Neidig says there's some indication that the conversion from female to male is based in part on the needs of the family group on a given reef. Where there are already lots of males, few females turn to males. Where there are few males, many of the females change sexes. The studies have already resulted in techniques that artificially bring on the female/male transition through hormone implantation.

RELEASING GROUPER

One of the side benefits of the Mote grouper study has been a catch-tag-release effort which is producing some interesting results. Mote researcher Karen Burns oversees this study.

"We are finding that the majority of grouper survive catch-and-release at depths up to 100 feet," says Burns. "This is true even if they come up with their eyes bulging and the stomach forced out the mouth by the change in air pressure. If the fish is put back over the side promptly, most of those fish will deflate and work their way back down."

She said that deflating the swim bladder improves survival in deeper water.

"In water over 100 feet deep, we found that survival was somewhat better for fish that were deflated, and over 150 feet not many survived that were not deflated."

She said that the best puncture device is a sharpened basketball needle inset into a small wood dowel, which acts as a handle. The needle is inserted in the side near the anal fin, and the stomach massaged gently to express the air.

"We know that fish treated this way survive because we re-catch many that are tagged, and also because we've studied them in the lab for months after they've been deflated," said Burns. "When we sacrifice a fish to examine for injury, we find a tiny, healed-over scar, so there's no long-term damage."

5

RED GROUPER

Red grouper, *Epinephelus morio,* are generally more abundant and more cooperative than gags. They don't reach the hulking sizes of their larger cousins, but they get big enough to put up a formidable battle, and they inhabit a niche in the Gulf strata that would otherwise be vacant. Reds average 4 to 8 pounds, and 10 to 15-pounders are not uncommon--though they're sure not as common as we might like them to be.

Typically, the average red is about 21 inches long when harvested, evidence that there's lots of pressure on the species, and that as soon as most exceed the minimum 20-inch legal size they take the one-way ride to the surface. By contrast, there are thousands of 19 3/4-inchers, and a typical day offshore in many areas might include catching 50 or more of these "shorts".

RED GROUPER HABITAT

Reds, unlike most reef species, prefer flat rock bottoms with holes for their hideaways--the "Swiss cheese" bottom described by divers is heaven to reds. Coral bottom, even if lacking major breaks, can also hold lots of reds. Along Florida's west coast most are caught from depths of 20 to 90 feet by the recreational fleet, with the majority of the catch taken between Sanibel and Tampa Bay over limestone bottom. Commercial boats also make good catches beyond the 20 fathom (120-foot) line, so there's no aversion to deep water in this species.

Find rocky bottom in 20 feet or more west of Marco and you'll find reds. Locals believe the fish move in closer during summer, often within 7 miles of the beach, and out farther in winter--the opposite pattern of gags, which seem to avoid hot water inshore in summer, and migrate landward in winter. There are lots of grouper fishermen in the area, and consequently most of the larger fish come from at least 25 miles out. The reef lines run generally north/south or northwest/southeast here, and when you pick up on a good break you can often follow it for miles by holding a compass heading as the rock rises out of the sand, then sinks back in. The average break is small, with the relief a couple of feet, but the area holds lots of fish.

On the Atlantic Coast, reds are often found deeper, too, along the edge of the 100- 150-foot ledges in the coral, with fishing best south of Florida's Port Canaveral. They're also common in the Bahamas.

Between Stuart and Ft. Pierce on Florida's east coast, fish move in to patch reefs almost on the beach in March and April. And the waters from Key West to the Dry Tortugas, historically a famed red grouper area, are coming back strongly thanks to the ban on fish traps there in 1992. The Marquesas Islands, 40 miles west of Key West, are particularly good. The fish are often found in water only 20 feet deep, which makes them good light tackle candidates.

In Florida Bay, the "bomb holes" south and west of Flamingo, with about 7-8 feet of water, often hold fish in late winter--or they did until recent water quality problems. If the flow from the Everglades is restored, these waters should remain productive.

You find reds mostly by finding hard bottom and then trolling. The obvious reefs, rockpiles and major breaks that hold gags and other species are less likely to hold reds. So it takes an

Red grouper are most abundant in the southeast Gulf, around the Florida Keys and along the Atlantic Shelf. The don't get quite as large as gags, and are generally found on less obvious reefs.

educated eye to pick out the change in bottom readout when the sonar signals bounce off flat rock instead of flat sand. Of course, at times you'll spot a ''Christmas tree'' that's a dead giveaway for a grouper hangout, but more often it's a matter of getting in the hard bottom zone, putting down a big diver-- on a downrigger or wire if the water is much over 20 feet--and pulling until something happens.

One trick that often works from October through May is to run to the stone-crab floats and troll these lines. Because stone crabs live in rocky bottom, these lines always mark likely grouper habitat. The traps go away when the season closes May 15, though. And top Gulf skippers like Capt. Dave Zalewski of Madeira Beach note that some big reds often cruise the area where a reef first rises out of the sand, as opposed to the main break.

Though reds are most often taken on cut bait, they readily tackle jigs bounced along reef edges.

Apparently these areas produce a forage that the reds like--or maybe it's a locale that's overlooked by boats that home in on the more obvious rock areas.

TACTICS FOR REDS

Red grouper are perhaps less cautious than gags, and they take cut bait just about as well as live baits. In fact, reds are less athletic than gags, as evidenced by their blocky shape, and they're consequently less inclined to run down fast-moving lures--the best trolling speed is usually just fast enough to bring out the action of the lure, around 4 knots. Trolling a live bait on a downrigger at even slower speeds is also a deadly tactic.

Because reds live on fairly flat bottom, it's possible to cast to them and get your rig back more often than you do when fishing sharp breaks where snags are just about a sure thing. Thus, fishing for reds doesn't require quite so much anchor-doctoring as fishing for gags or snapper.

In fact, a stout spinning rig loaded with 25-pound-test makes a good red grouper rig, where that's underweight by half for big gags. And reds lend themselves to casting artificials, with 3 to 8 ounce bucktail jigs tipped with a florescent plastic worm the best bet. Don't be afraid to offer them the larger sizes--if the bait doesn't bang off bottom, they usually won't take it, so you need plenty of weight to get down. And even a 3-pounder will tackle a half-pound jig trailing an 8-inch plastic tail. Adding a mullet strip or a small ballyhoo will double the number of strikes most days.

MANAGEMENT

Red grouper females reach sexual maturity at 19 to 20 inches, at which they are likely to be 6 to 7 years old. With such a slow maturity, it's clear that overfishing the stocks would be easy--something that was happening before the 20-inch size limit went into place.

The spawn is strongest in April and May in the Gulf. Reds don't get as large as gags, with the typical 10-year-old red about 22 inches long compared to almost 32 inches long for a 10-year-old gag. However, at a given size reds tend to be heavier than gags due to their deeper body profile. The current IGFA record is 39 pounds 8 ounces taken off Port Canaveral, Florida. (The gag record, on the other hand, is 80 pounds, 6 ounces, caught in the Gulf of Mexico off Destin.)

Reds tend to be a bit less active than the more streamlined and vigorous gags, and depend more on camouflage rather than speed for protection. Like other closely related Epinephelus species, they can quickly change colors to match surroundings.

Reds are known to aggregate for spawning and sometimes for feeding. There's a reported feed in November near Lower Matecumbe, in the Florida Keys, that includes hundreds if not thousands of fish. These fish clearly do some moving to gather, so the species does migrate on occasion, but tends to stay within a home zone rather closely once settled in new surroundings.

Because they're not usually long-distance swimmers, reds are also highly susceptible to red tide, the microscopic organism that builds up to toxic levels in summer along much of Florida's southwest coast. In some cases, entire populations have been wiped out by the tide, a natural disaster that, thus far, has never figured into management calculations. A red tide in the late 1950's reportedly killed most of the red grouper from Tampa Bay southward, and for years afterward most anglers caught only gags, while prior to that date reds had been the predominate species. It remains to be seen what the effect of the widespread red tides during the summer of 1995 will have on the fishery, but thousands of reds died as a result.

The introduction of loran brought in the "golden age" of recreational bottom fishing, which lasted through the 70's as many sport fishermen found they could catch enough grouper and snapper to pay for their boats. Naturally, as the number of boats with electronic gear built up, the crash of the resource eventually came, and by the mid-1980's, most reef anglers were having a tough time finding grouper more than 20 inches long. Things only began to improve when Florida's Marine Fisheries Commission, accompanied by howls of protest from both sportfishermen and commercials, put a 20-inch limit in place for both reds and gags. Like many other conservative management

6

RED SNAPPER

Red snapper are the glamour species of bottom fishing, at least among the restaurant crowd. *Lutjanus campechanus* has a well-deserved reputation as a super table fish, and that has made it a target for both commercial and recreational anglers for over 100 years.

Ironically, red snapper is probably not the best-tasting of all bottom-dwellers--that honor most likely goes to the rather rare and beautiful but unfortunately-named hogfish, sometimes called a hog snapper though it's actually a member of the wrasse family. But a prime "chicken" red of 4 to 8 pounds is assuredly a match for yellowtails, mangrove snapper or pretty much anything else the sea has to offer.

And the large average size of red snapper and their abundance makes them a great target for recreational anglers. As high as 8 million pounds have been harvested annually in recent years from U.S. waters by the combined recreational and commercial hook-and-line fisheries, making this one of the most caught and most valuable of all reef-dwellers. (At that, fishing is nothing like it once was--early boats reported catches of 10,000 pounds daily when the banks off Campeche, Mexico, were first discovered in the early 1900's!)

Kate Phillips shows a nice red snapper taken off Orange Beach, Alabama. A jig bounced on deep structure did the job. (John Phillips Photo)

Reds are best distinguished from similar snappers by their overall pink color, their reddish eye and by the long pectoral fins. The average fish goes around 5 pounds, but they're commonly caught to the upper 20's and low 30's. The world record is 46 pounds, 8 ounces, caught off Destin, Florida in 1985. The range is roughly from the Carolinas around the tip of Florida and throughout the Gulf of Mexico. A closely related species is also caught throughout the Caribbean.

The adults are always found close to bottom structure, while the juveniles are more common over near-shore mud bottoms. The biggest fish are usually found in more than 100 feet of water, and they're commonly caught out to at least 400 feet.

WHERE TO FIND THEM

In Florida waters, they're more common from Sebastian's Inlet northward than to the south, mainly because fish traps decimated populations farther south and the numbers have not yet recovered. Historically there was an excellent fishery off the Dry Tortugas, and it's showing signs of recovery since the trap ban in the early 1990's.

In the Gulf the best catches are in the northern sector, off the panhandle and extending west off Alabama, Mississippi, Louisiana and Texas in water depths of 200 feet and more. The oil rig country around the Mississippi Delta and westward is all good, with lots of small "chicken" snapper to 6 pounds on the inshore rigs, bigger "sows" 20 pounds and up on those most distant from land.

Off the beaches of north Florida and Alabama, there's a major amateur reef-building program, with local skippers trucking old appliances, tires, steel drums and other structure out to make their own mini-reefs. This sort of small, secret structure frequently becomes home to lunker snapper. Many anglers sink a reef and let it set for three or four years so that fish can find it and grow up there before they drop the first hook.

SNAPPER TACTICS

Like all snappers, reds are somewhat difficult to hook, though their larger mouths make it possible for them easily to take a whole squid or a baitfish up to six inches long. They're not inclined to freight-train a bait like a big gag grouper, but when a live bait is lowered to their depth they usually latch on with vigor.

61

Tin squids or jigging spoons also work well on red snapper. The compact shape of these lures gets them deep in a hurry. (John Phillips Photo)

One of the best baits is the common scaled sardine found inshore. The baits don't last long when sent down a couple hundred feet at crash-dive speed, but they don't have to--if they so much as wiggle over an active reef, they get eaten. Anglers net these baits over the grass flats in coastal bays, and add threadfins found along the beaches. Scooping up fresh squid under the lights before morning also adds to the bait well, if you can keep the crew from converting this part of your stock to calamari.

Captain Joe Penovich of Port Canaveral, Florida, specializes in sow snapper there, and he likes live spot and live pinfish fished on 7/0 to 9/0 short-shank Mustad hooks for the big ones. For smaller reds, he prefers fresh or frozen herring on 5/0's. Penovich says fishing in his area is best December through March at depths of 80 to 240 feet. Best tip for beginning snapper fishermen trying these depths?

"Don't set the hook," says Penovich. "With that much line out, no matter how hard you set you'll only move the hook a couple inches, just enough to jerk the bait out of the fish's mouth. The best thing to do is just start reeling. When the line comes tight the fish takes off and that usually jerks the barb home."

Reds put up a spirited fight until they're cranked out of their depth zone, at which time expansion of the air bladder puts an end to the fight. The same tackle that's commonly used for grouper farther inshore works fine for red snapper: 6'6" rods like the Penn Senator[R] 3145 ARW armed with a 112 or 113 series Senator[R] reel and 50-pound-test will do the job. In the deeper water of his area, Captain Penovich likes a 114H Senator[R] with a 7-foot rod and 80-pound-test mono. And at depths over 250 feet you're into electric reel country, without which fishing gets to be a whole lot like work.

Reds can be at least as finicky as the other snapper, particularly in clear water, and when they are a switch to lighter gear may be needed. Captain Robert Trosset, who chases reds off the Dry Tortugas, says conditions there sometimes require dropping back to 30-pound gear in order to get the fish to bite. Trosset says that reds are gradually coming back to the area since fish traps were banned, but that the great fishing of the past is still a couple years away as this is written.

Reds are most abundant in the western Gulf, where every oil rig and wreck has plenty. However, the largest fish usually don't come from these hard-fished spots, but from remote areas of hard bottom and tiny home-built artificial reefs where the fish can survive long enough to reach lunker size, 20 pounds and up. Top skippers "motorfish" these spots, holding position over the locale marked on the depthfinder while anglers send whole cigar minnows or other whole baits down to the fish. The philosophy is that cut bait won't make it through the junk fish long enough for a big red to find it, so fresh, whole baits are

Monsters like this are rare, but expert skippers still manage to find them in the deep Gulf and along the 100-200-foot drop in the Atlantic. Live baits and 6/0 tackle are best for lunker reds. (John Phillips Photo)

the way to go. Here as elsewhere, the fish bite best at night, with full moon nights maybe the best of the best.

Reds have always been money fish, and before recreational limits were put in place, many "sport" fishermen literally paid for their offshore boats with their snapper catches, sometimes hauling up over $2,000 in "red gold" daily. For years, several boats out of Daytona worked a giant spring and made hundreds of thousands of dollars on the snapper--until, surprise!--they depleted the fishery.

SNAPPER CONSERVATION

The major problem for red snapper in most areas, though, is not fishing pressure but shrimping pressure. In the northern and western gulf, where red snapper are most abundant, shrimp trawls capture more than 80 percent of the juveniles in some areas. Fisheries scientists have known this for years, but the powerful lobbying of the big money the shrimp catch generates has thus far managed to prevent rules from being put in place to protect these young fish.

Of course, it's an arguable point: should fish managers put added strictures on the most lucrative fishery in the Gulf to protect a very limited finfish fishery, at least in terms of recreational fishing? But the best management pretty clearly would be one that combines a finfish excluder device (a FED, to make it acronymically similar to the TED shrimpers must now use) to shuck out the juvenile fish that make up about 90 percent of the shrimpers haul in many areas. That way, the shrimpers could continue to harvest the shrimp everybody loves, and we'd also restore the snapper populations.

The problem, thus far, is finding a FED that doesn't allow too many shrimp to escape along with the fish. Hopefully, researchers will come up with a device that does the job to everybody's satisfaction in the near future, assuring better snapper fishing as well as plenty of shrimp kabobs.

7

MANGO'S, INSHORE AND OFF

They're pitbulls with fins.

An attitude in scales.

Mangrove snapper are possibly the species which gave the snapper clan its name--these snappers snap. Once they latch on, they hold like snapping turtles.

And, with spiked canine teeth, ''mangos'' get the attention of whatever they snap on to.

Mangrove snapper--actually gray snapper, *Lutjanus griseus*-- are one of only a few species of fish that will wait patiently on the hook for an angler to stick an errant finger too close to their jaws, then lash out sideways like an alligator and grab hold.

The only release is to pry open the jaws--when they connect, they seem to take a wild joy in watching the victim dance and howl. Of course, you can't blame the snapper for self-defense. If it weren't for one very pleasant fact about these very unpleasant fish, most people would stay well clear of them.

But mangrove snappers taste great. In fact, they may be even more delectable than their famed offshore cousins, the red snapper. Their meat is lighter and more delicate than the big reds. Adult mangroves usually migrate offshore, where they're called gray snapper, but it's still the same species, identified by the gray to

Mangrove or gray snapper are aggressive both in attacking baits and in defending themselves, and have sharp teeth to help out on both counts.

green scales, reddish fins and two very pronounced upper canine teeth.

Young fish to about 3 pounds are abundant in inshore waters where anglers fishing from small boats, bridges and even from shore can find them. They come by the "mangrove" nickname honestly, because the little ones often prowl oyster-encrusted roots along steep shorelines.

According to the National Marine Fisheries Service, young snapper grow about 4 inches per year in their first two years, about 3 inches per year the next two years, and about 2 inches a year through age 6 for the few that survive that long, reaching around 17 inches. The world record is an outsized 17 pounder, caught off Port Canaveral.

Like most snappers, the females are caught more often inshore, the males more often offshore. Most females are sexually mature at age 2 and a length of around 7.5 inches, while males mature at around the same age and a length of about 7.3 inches. Mature females are usually larger than mature males. The mangroves spawn from June through August, with the young floating as zooplankton until they settle into suitable inshore cover around mangroves and grass flats.

MANGOS IN TAMPA BAY

Captain Jerry Williams of Tampa is among a small group of guides who targets mangroves in Tampa Bay.

"There have always been mangrove snapper in Old Hillsborough Bay," Williams told me, "but the last few years there have been more of them, and they've been bigger. I think it's because the water has cleaned up and there's more bait up here now."

Williams said the fish show up in August, and fishing remains good throughout the winter.

While the snapper most anglers catch are under the legal 10" limit, Williams uses tactics that seem to attract larger fish, with the average 12 to 14 inches long.

LIVE BAIT TIPS

"You can catch big snapper on shrimp, but the most consistent bait is live sardines," Williams said. "I think that fluttering bait brings out their nasty nature and they just belt it."

However, he notes that the big scaled sardines preferred by snook fishermen are not the ticket for snapper.

"If a bait is longer than 4 inches, most bay mango's can't get it in their mouth. They might knock it off the hook, but they can't swallow it on that first strike, so you don't very often hook them. Smaller sardines that snook fishermen would throw away is what you need for snapper."

Williams catches his bait in the lower sections of Hillsborough Bay by chumming with the classic mix of jack mackerel, sardines in oil, whole wheat bread and anise oil. His bait net is different than most, however.

"I had a special net made up to catch this small bait without gilling it," Williams told me. "The mesh is 3/16, and that won't gill even a 2-inch sardine." He doesn't use 2-inchers on the hook, but notes that they make great live chum.

"Snapper are just like snook, you need to get them started a lot of times with some live chum. I throw a couple of handfuls out and when they start popping it on the surface, I know they're ready to bite."

He says the fish are generally found around rocky ledges, rubble on channel drops, points and anywhere else where bottom structure provides reef-like hiding areas. The bait is fished on 1/0 or 2/0 hooks, and is hooked just above the pectoral fin.

"Hooking a bait through the nose allows it to just hang in the current, and that doesn't turn snapper on a lot of times," Williams said. "Hooked in the pecs, they flutter sideways and shine in the water, and the fish can't stand that."

On a trip I made with Williams not long ago, we drew a zero on the first stop, but on the second location where Jerry anchored, his chum drew immediate surface explosions. Both our sardines promptly disappeared in surface boils when we flipped them near the rocky shoreline.

The fish powered for the rocks, pulling drag like miniature snook as they tried to get back to their hiding places. Williams advises anglers to use 10- to 12-pound test spinning gear, and to keep the drag locked down to near the breaking strength of the line--otherwise, many fish reach the rubble and cut off.

We finally pulled them near enough for the guide to net-- a pair of stocky 2-pounders that came up with their jaws audibly popping. Williams wisely made use of a pair of very long-nosed pliers to remove the hooks.

My next cast drew another nice snapper, but Williams found his fish had bigger shoulders--it ripped off drag and headed for the open channel. The fish waltzed around William's big aluminum boat three times before boiling up on top--a redfish over 30 inches long. The fish saved us the task of releasing it when it dived under the boat and clipped the line.

We also caught several small snook and ladyfish as well as lots more snapper before a pair of porpoises moved in and put every fish in the hole down.

We motored on, stopping here and there around spoil islands and throughout the shipping channels of downtown Tampa,

Mangroves are often found along the rocky edges of ship channels. They move to inshore waters in cool weather, and often bite well in bays and coastal rivers. Those fish caught inside average a couple of pounds--larger ones are rare.

picking up two or three fish on some spots, none on others. Some locations had only snook, some only snapper, some jacks, some a potpourri of everything in the upper bay.

"The nice thing about this fishing is that it's close to home, and that it just keeps on getting better as the water cools," Williams told me as we finished off our five-fish limit on snapper.

DEEP WATER MANGOS

Larger mangroves, 4 to 6 pounds, prefer deeper water. Many are caught on the same offshore reefs that hold gag grouper, in water as much as 100 feet deep, and these fish are nearly always labeled "gray" snapper by the offshore headboats. There are also good numbers of them on the edges of most major shipping channels in areas such as Tampa Bay, with fishing particularly good in these areas September through November. Here, there's a 20-foot break, where the bay bottom at 25 feet is dredged away to the channel at 45 feet. And lower Tampa Bay also holds mangos on the many artificial reefs built from the old Skyway Bridge.

Off Weeki Wachee, the fish move into inshore rocks in 12 to 15 feet of water August through early October, where they can be chummed to the surface with live sardines and caught on light tackle with free-lined baits.

Mangroves also gather on the reefs of the Florida Keys in July, apparently to spawn, and can provide super fishing when you find the aggregations. Like other snapper, these clear water fish bite best early and late in the day, as well as after dark.

In deep water these fish are usually caught with light grouper tackle, which is to say 30- to 40-pound tackle and lead weights of about 3-4 ounces. The basic difference between snappering and groupering is that snapper are more likely to take a bait that's presented 5 feet or more off the bottom, while the grouper usually like the bait swimming very close to the structure. The best snapper anglers let the bait hit bottom, then take up a couple of turns on the reel to give them the right distance off the cover.

When the water is clear, you may have to go lighter, using 20-pound gear and 1-ounce sinkers and rigging the bait on hooks no larger than size 1. This light rig won't hit bottom unless you wait for slack tide periods, but when you get it down, it catches fish. In the keys, many anglers move down to yellowtail gear to catch mangroves--light spinning tackle, quarter-sized bits of bait and lots of chum does the job. And experts like Robert Trosset say that if you see fish but they won't bite, go to lighter leader material--in extreme cases, anglers may have to try fishing leader testing only 12 pounds in order to fool the suspicious mangos.

RIVER MANGOS

Like many other fish species that frequent inshore waters, a good number of mangrove snapper push into coastal rivers and shipping basins during cold weather. These fish settle into rocky holes, and are readily caught on live shrimp drifted near bottom with just enough weight to keep it down. Every coastal river along the Gulf Coast has lots of mango's from November through February, as does the Cross Florida Barge Canal.

When they're in the rivers, the snapper expect baits to be moving with the flow, so it often pays to fish a shrimp like an artificial, tossing it upcurrent, letting it drift down through the holes, then retrieving and making another cast. A bait anchored to bottom won't catch many mangroves.

On the other side of the coin, there's also a run of mangroves into the flats of Florida Bay in July. The fishing there can be especially interesting because the mango's sometimes follow stingrays, making sight-casting with topwaters and even flyrod streamers a possibility. Another way to locate these fish is to keep an eye out for white sandholes in water 8 to 10 feet deep. These are areas that usually have a bit of rocky structure in the center, and fish working in and out of the rocks have cleaned away all the grass. You anchor uptide of the spot and pitch lightly weighted shrimp, small baitfish or fresh-cut bait to the fish.

DOCK SNAPPER

Mangroves are also the notorious "dock snapper" of the Florida Keys. These PhD's of fishdom are often seen but rarely caught, and are noted for the microscopic inspection of every bit of bait tossed at them to check for hooks.

The only good way to catch them from the dock is to crawl out on your belly and present a bait on light line, without ever rising high enough off the deck that they can spot you. It also works occasionally to stand on shore well away from the dock and present a free-lined shrimp or live sardine with a long cast.

A better approach is to anchor a boat within casting distance, preferably at dawn or dusk, and toss unweighted live baits to the structure. Around docks with fish-cleaning tables, sometimes bits of cut fish will do better than shrimp. And you can always sweeten the pot by chumming with fish parts, a few live shrimp or a handful of dizzied sardines. Big secret is to use no weight at all--let the bait drift down naturally on a size 1 or 1/0 hook and a leader testing no more than 15 pounds.

Dock snapper are among the most difficult of all fish to catch, but with patience and the right approach, you can always convert at least a few of these smart-alecks into fillets.

8

MUTTONS AND YELLOWTAILS

There are dozens of varieties of snapper other than red and mangroves of interest to anglers, but the two most common are muttons and yellowtails, both primarily tropic species found from Florida waters south and east into the Bahamas. These snapper are most commonly found within reasonable distance from shore, and even on the inshore flats in the case of the mutton, making them a popular target for small boat fishermen using light tackle. Here's a closer look:

MUTTON SNAPPER

Is the mutton snapper, *Lutjanus analis,* a flats fish or a reef fish? It's best known on the flats of the Florida Keys, where many anglers consider it the ultimate trophy, the smartest, most wary and toughest of all shallow-water adversaries. The typical mutton on the flats goes 8 to 10 pounds, but the world record is 28 pounds, 5 ounces. Muttons have reddish bars on their lower body and red tails, with the back tan or green. There's also a prominent black spot on the back, about 2/3 of the way to the tail.

Muttons, like other snappers, favor rocky bottom and deeper water, and that's where the majority spend most of their time. The reefs out to at least 200 feet are their normal habitat, and they also frequent rocky channels and patch reefs close inshore

This mutton was caught on the flats near Key West from a bass boat. The species often prowls water only knee deep, though it's more abundant on offshore reefs.

throughout the Keys. But the mutton causes the most excitement when it prowls knee-deep water during the cooler months, looking for shrimp and crabs in the turtle grass. When they do, they're susceptible to sight-fishing with tipped jigs, crab-imitation flies and live shrimp or baitfish.

Muttons are very cautious when they're on the flats, at least as spooky as bonefish, and catching one on fly is seen as a feat comparable to landing a permit on the long rod. When hooked, they make powerful and very rapid runs and generally conduct themselves in premiere gamefish style.

While the muttons that come on the flats get most of the attention, the muttons that come to the patch reefs around the keys, mostly in fall and winter, are the ones most frequently caught. Anglers drift between the keys and the outer reefs in 8 to 20 feet of water with mullet chunks, ballyhoo or other cut bait, or with live pinfish, 'hoo or blue crab around small outcroppings. Another good tactic is to anchor up and let the current carry chum to the reef, which lures the fish to within casting range. This works best with clear and calm waters, because in those conditions approaching too close to a reef is likely to put the muttons off their feed.

Most anglers use 30-pound baitcasting gear for this approach, or stout spinning tackle with 25-pound-test, needed to have any hope of holding a 15-pounder out of the rocks.

Lots of mutton snapper are also caught on deeper reefs, especially around the full moon periods in summer, at water depths of 100 to 130 feet both in the keys and north to Stuart. They're a lot less cautious at these depths, and readily grab a 4 to 6 ounce jig trimmed with a fluttering 8-inch tail of bonito belly or even a florescent plastic worm. Many anglers also score by drifting with the current just at the edge of the reef while trailing a ballyhoo "plug" made by cutting off the head and tail of the baitfish, then burying a tandem-rig hook into it. Egg sinkers between 2 and 6 ounces keep the bait in contact with bottom.

Muttons are among the tastiest of all reef fish, and are delicious any way you cook them.

YELLOWTAIL SNAPPER

This colorful snapper, *Ocyurus chrysurus*, averages 1 to 3 pounds but reaches a maximum of at least 8 pounds, 8 ounces, the current IGFA record. The bright yellow tail and yellow stripe down the side make it easy to identify. It's the favorite snapper around the Florida Keys and north along the Atlantic Coast of Florida to Stuart. It's most often found in water less than 150 feet deep. Due to years of warm weather, the species appears to be abundant in the central Gulf at present, with strong catches being reported off St. Petersburg at times.

The most effective tactic is chumming with glass minnows over the reefs. Ground fish mixed with dog food, oats or other fillers also works, and many anglers add a dollop of menhaden oil to the mix to make the slick spread.

One of the more effective chumming tactics is to make a "bomb" of wet sand, fish bits and menhaden oil with minnows mixed in. A handful of this sinks rapidly, taking the minnows down with it to snapper country.

Some yellowtails can be caught by day, yet they bite ten times better after sundown. And it's usually necessary even then to use light tackle and minimal weight to fool them. Small live baitfish are effective, and they will take bits of fresh cut fish when chummed strongly. Best tackle is spinning gear like Penn's 5500 SS reel and a Power Stick(R) fiberglass rod or Power Graph(R) graphite composite rod with 8- to 12-pound-test mono, size 1 to 1/0 hooks, and very small sinkers, about 1/8 ounce, so that the bait sinks slowly through fish rising to the chum.

Another tactic is to make a sandball around a chunk of bait, then wrap the ball with about 6 feet of the running line to hold it together long enough for the mass to sink. By the time it hits bottom water has dispersed the sand and chum and the uncovered bait is in the strike zone. (You have to wash your hands after making each sandball before you pick up your reel--otherwise, grit gets inside and causes problems.) Sandballing is used when only small 'tails are coming to the top, or when undesirable species are beating the larger snapper to the baits.

Yellowtails are bottom-dwellers, but they rise to the surface more readily than most reef species when chummed. It's common to catch them on free-lined live baits once you have them turned on and working near the top.

Yellowtails usually hang over reefs that are home to larger species including black grouper, and a favorite charterboat tactic is to hook a small 'tail on a big rig and lower it down under the fish working the chum to lure these giants. (Remember, yellowtails have to be at least 12 inches long to be in possession, though, and the Marine Patrol considers using one for bait ''possessing'', so measure before you bait up.)

'Tails spawn in mid-summer, and they gather by the hundreds over the reef lines in the Keys and southeastern Florida around the full moon in July. Fishing can be good year around in moderate weather, but if you can make only one yellowtail trip a year, make it in midsummer.

9

GIANTS OF THE REEFS

While most grouper and snapper fall into the 8- to 20-pound class, there are some true giants of the reef clan that are less rarely caught but so impressive when they take the hook that they qualify as big game fish, on a par with the tunas and wahoos for the back-breaking battles they can provide. These monsters require different baits, different tackle--and a different attitude to bring them to the boat. Here's a look at these linemen of the sea:

BLACK GROUPER

Mycteroperca bonaci, true black grouper, have a black body with white jigsaw mottling. Gags are commonly mislabled black grouper, but the true black has a richer black color and more nearly white patterning, while gags tend to be deep gray mottled with lighter gray and brown. Blacks are a more tropical species than the gag, and are usually found farther offshore in the Gulf, farther south in the Atlantic. They reach a larger average size, as well, with 25-pounders common. The current IGFA record is 113 lb 6 oz. caught off the Dry Tortugas in 1990.

They bite any sort of live bait, and the big boys, 30 pounds and up, readily attack baits more than a foot long. Blacks are fast and aggressive, and have been seen running down bonito in the open sea--a bit of a rush, even for a marlin! Fishing is best along the southeast coast of Florida in winter, when the fish move to the inshore reefs. Trolling a boned mullet over the reefs from Key Biscayne southward often lures them up, and many anglers believe that a fast speed, around 6 knots, draws more hits than the typical 4-knot tow used for less active grouper. A good tactic is to troll the inside of the main reef at the edge of the drop with Magnum Rapalas or similar divers on the south legs, with your lures probing around 20 feet, then turn and work the outside edge, where water is 50 to 100 feet deep, with a downrigger and spoon on north legs.

When you find fish, you may do even better drifting with large, live blue runners over reefs 40 to 60 feet deep--some anglers sink the baits down about 30 feet on downriggers. Capt. Robert Trosset of Key West, maybe Florida's top black grouper skipper, says his favorite live bait for this work is a big yellowtail, at least two pounds.

"I've seen them turn down a 1-pound bait, and you put one twice as big down there and they can't leave it alone," says Trosset. "I've even caught some on 4-pound yellowtails--except I can't very often convince a customer to put down a snapper that nice to catch a grouper!"

Bouncing large jigs on the edge of the 150-foot drop also works. Trosset says he likes a 4-ounce jig with a trailer hook, sometimes two trailers, buried in a ballyhoo. His favorite drifting area is water 150 to 210 feet deep between Sand Key and Cosgrove Light, along the outer edges of the reefs outside Hawk Channel.

And when the fish move into the shallows, a few anglers even hook up by tossing monster surface plugs like the Arbogast Scudder and "balooping" the fish to the top.

JEWFISH

Epinephelus itajara is the true giant of the grouper clan, with reliable reports of 700-pound fish exceeding eight feet long. The

Big black grouper like this one are powerful, aggressive gamefish willing to run down big baits in the open ocean. Blacks are most common in southwest Florida and the Caribbean

IGFA record is 680 pounds, taken off Fernandina Beach, Fla., in 1961. Jewfish are identified by the tan/yellow body with olive or dark brown vertical bands, rounded tail, and the sprinkle of small spots over much of the head and body. They're found throughout Florida waters, but are most common where there are inshore mangroves, roughly the southern half of the state. Apparently the juveniles make extensive use of mangrove shallows until they mature. They grow rapidly. The average 100-pounder is about 4 feet long, and at 5 feet most have exceeded 200 pounds. They're known to live at least 35 years.

These slow-moving groupers haven't done well in the age of coastal development and the spear gun, and are now so rare that no harvest is allowed. They still show up on the flats of the Keys in summer, settling into deep holes and cuts where they occasionally scare the bejeezus out of bonefish anglers.

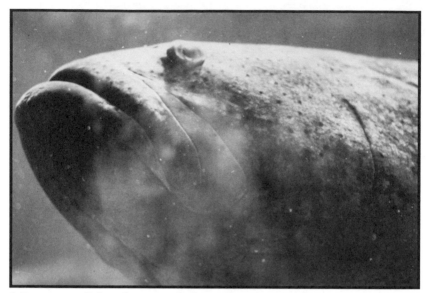

Monsters like this jewfish make up the heavyweights of the reef clan. They reach weights in excess of 700 pounds. They're often found in passes and even in tidal creeks as well as on shallow reefs.

In the old days, Keys anglers used to fish from the U.S. 1 bridges with 5-pound jacks as bait, rigged to the cable-winches on the front of their Jeeps. There is a legend, possibly true, that a CJ was actually pulled to the railing by a monster jewfish (or maybe a big hammerhead) before the cable snapped. Another noted jewfish hole was the phosphate dock at Boca Grande, still a good spot if you just want the experience of pulling on a "grouper" big enough to swallow you whole.

Jewfish are most often found in water under 100 feet deep, and they're the only one of the groupers that actually seems to prefer inshore habitat to offshore reefs. A current stronghold is the Sunshine Skyway Bridge, which spans the mouth of Tampa Bay. There, underwater structure, high current flow and an endless supply of bait make great jewfish habitat.

Another spot for catch-and-release jewfishing is Everglades National Park, where they are reasonably abundant in the deeper rivers flowing out of the back country. Find a rocky hole with water more than 8 feet deep and drift a big live bait through it and you may be rewarded with a tug-of-war with a hundred pounder. (The tactic also hooks tarpon and giant snook, so it can be productive whether you find the J-fish or not.)

Researchers report that large individuals settle into one home base and live there for years, moving only during the spawn. The species spawns in summer, and spawning aggregations have been observed by divers over wrecks in depths of about 100-120 feet. The stay-put habit makes depletion by red tide a danger for the species, and also makes them very susceptible to overfishing. As a result, the season has been closed since 1990.

WARSAW GROUPER

Epinephelus nigritus has an overall deep gray or black coloration with occasional white mottling. They're most common along the edge of the continental shelf, and on other reefs where depth exceeds 100 feet. Rumors of 800 pounders are apparently only that, but these fish definitely get big. Scientists have aged warsaws to 41 years, at which the length was almost 92 inches-- imagine, if you can, a grouper nearly 8 feet long! The IGFA record is 436 pounds, 12 ounces, taken off Destin, Florida in 1985. What does a warsaw eat? Anything he wants to. Lobster and all sorts of smaller fish are fodder. As with the other large groupers, the trick to catching a warsaw is to think big--a bait of 3 to 5 pounds is not excessive.

CUBERA SNAPPER

When you talk about fish with an attitude, the cubera snapper, *Lutjanus cyanopterus*, is one of the bad boys. Imagine a mangrove snapper that weighs 100 pounds and up and you get a picture of how a cubera looks and how it behaves. They have big, nasty

Kite fishing a live blue runner or a yellowtail along the reef line is a good way to draw up a big black. The same bait in the same spot also works for winter kings and sailfish.

canines and they are inclined to attack anything that will fit into their mouths.

Off the west coast of Panama a few years back, I was reeling in a Pacific barracuda about 3 feet long when a big red-brown shadow rose out of 200 feet of water and inhaled the catch. The yard-long cuda went down the throat of that cubera like it was a shiner in the mouth of a bass, just "WHOOMP" and it was gone. That's about how long my line lasted, too, when the fish headed back for bottom. (Pacific cuberas are very similar to Atlantic cuberas, but don't get quite as large--this one was only the size of a 55-gallon oil drum.)

Cuberas in the Atlantic reach at least 125 pounds, though the recognized IGFA record is 121 pounds, 8 ounces, caught in the Gulf off Cameron, LA. They're not often caught, but a few guys out of south Florida ports from Stuart through the Keys do specialize in them, particularly during the strong bite around the full moons of July and August. They're also taken in winter at "The Elbow", about a hundred miles west of St. Petersburg, Florida and just south of the famed Middle Grounds grouper area.

Best bait? Get this--live spiny lobster. Not me--if I've got a spiny lobster, I'm going to eat it myself, not waste it on a snapper. But if you want a big cubera, this is the ticket. The bait is usually double-hooked so it won't be lost, one hook under the shell at the horn on the head, as with live shrimp, and one into the shell at the tail, with 300-pound mono or heavy wire between. (I'd be inclined to quadruple hook it, at the price of crawfish!) Some anglers use a double-hook jig of 9 to 12 ounces or a jig with a stinger. During the closed season on crawfish, large live blue crabs also work well, as do live yellowtail snapper.

They bite best at night, like all snappers, and they're usually found along the edge of the outer reef lines, between 100 and 200 feet. Expert anglers like Capt. Mike Houghtaling and Capt. Bouncer Smith of Miami advise drift-fishing the drops, rather than anchoring, and also say that making too much noise over the fish can put them down, even at 200-foot depths.

Because of the large size of the fish and their inclination to dive into cover, very heavy gear is standard--something like the 114 Penn Senator(R) 6/0 mounted on a solid glass 3160RW Senator(R) Rod and loaded with 80- to 100-pound-test mono. Terminal gear is also massive, with 10/0 forged hooks and 130-pound test braided cable leader standard. It's brutal tackle for a brutal but challenging fish, the most senior of the snappers.

Like most of the giants of the reef, cubera are best caught for the sport of the battle rather than for their fillets. The flesh is coarse, and because these fish are so far up the food chain, chances of ciguetera are high. It's best to exercise them and then turn them loose to grow even bigger.

10

OTHER REEF SPECIES

There are dozens of other reef species, including grouper and snapper strains less commonly caught by U.S. anglers but still abundant enough to allow targeted fishing in many areas. Here's a look at some of the most popular:

SCAMP

The scamp, *Mycteroperca phenax*, is identified by whips on the tailfin and anal fin. The overall color is a deep rust, with lighter mottling in young fish. They're commonly found in 50 to 300 feet off the Carolinas--a major fishery--along Florida's Atlantic coast and throughout the Gulf. Like gags, scamp prefer big ledges rather than smaller structure. They're apparently long-lived--biologists recorded a 21-year-old off South Carolina. The fish measured about 35 inches long. The current record is 28 pounds, taken off Port Canaveral. At 20 inches, scamp weigh around 5.5 pounds. Scamp are usually more wary than gag and reds and so less often caught. A lively sardine or threadfin is a hard bait to beat.

NASSAU GROUPER

Once a common species off south Florida, *Epinephelus striatus* has been overfished and had to be removed from the legal harvest list. Nassau's look similar to red grouper in body

Three at a time! Black sea bass don't get big, but they're so abundant and cooperative that they make excellent targets on days when the other reef species are hard to find. Small jigs, shrimp or cut bait does the job.

shape, but have a deeper red/brown color, lighter vertical bands instead of random splotches, and a black saddle in front of the tail. Not surprisingly, they're most abundant in the Bahamas, where they're readily caught by trolling the reefs with diving plugs. A nice thing about fishing the islands is that you don't need a depthfinder to locate productive fish habitat--it's readily visible in the clear water at depths down to 70 feet. And fish will chase a lure a long way in such clear water--if the plug passes within 20 feet of the structure, it will draw attention.

YELLOWFIN GROUPER

Mycteroperca venenosa is common around the Bahamas, Jamaica, Bermuda and Central America, and a few are also caught deep in the Gulf of Mexico. It has a reddish body with brown mottling and distinctive yellow edges on pectoral fin. Deep water fish are more red, shallow water fish tend to be green-brown. It's one of the most active grouper, able to run down fast-moving species like bar jack. The species reaches lengths of about 3 feet, and the IGFA record is 34 lbs., 6 oz., landed at Largo, Fla. Best fishing is around the reefs of the Bahamas in 30 to 70 feet of water, where the yellowfins attack diving plugs towed next to the coral heads and also grab jigs tipped with ballyhoo or other fish. In some areas, the species has a high incidence of ciguetera.

BLACK SEA BASS

In southern waters, black sea bass, *Centropristis striata*, are what you catch when you can't catch anything else. They're the consolation prize, not very big, not very glamorous, but very abundant. The species is more admired north of Cape Hatteras, where it's known as "blackfish" and where the average fish is larger. There's a tie for the world record, with both 9-pound, 8-ounce fish caught near Virginia Beach. There's a strong headboat fishery off Long Island, NY, with a surge in November and December, a time when fans say your spit freezes before it hits the deck! Along with grunts, it's the most commonly-caught fish on inshore partyboats throughout much of the southeast.

North or south, black sea bass are numerous over many types of hard bottom strata. The average size is no more than a pound, but locate a rock that's holding mature spawners in spring and you may deck lots of fish over 2 to 3 pounds. These are large, purple-black hump-backs that almost appear to be a different species from the much smaller and lighter-colored juveniles.

Blacks take just about anything that will fit into their ample mouths, including shrimp, cut bait, small baitfish and an assortment of small jigs and lead spoons. The only requirement is to get the offering down to their terrain, within a few feet of bottom.

A plus for Gulf anglers is that they're as abundant on deep grass flats as farther offshore, and often a grouper trip that comes up empty can be salvaged by a short stop over the grass in water 6 to 12 feet deep, where a 3/8 ounce jig tipped with a bit of shrimp will always produce a dozen of these panfish in short order. And, when it comes to the table, most who have tried sea bass would throw away a plate of grouper fingers in favor of them. The flesh is white, moist and tender. It has a flavor that is approached by few other fish, with the possible exception of hog snapper.

Most bottom fishermen don't have much respect for sea bass because a 2-pound fish on 50-pound tackle doesn't give much of an account of itself. But catch that same fish on 8-pound spinning tackle--easy to do when the fish are found in their usual haunts in less than 20 feet of water throughout the northeastern Gulf--and you have a very respectable fighter that is also extremely cooperative.

Black sea bass grow at about the same rate as the groupers in their first year, reaching about 6 inches and a weight of around a quarter-pound. However, by the second year they lag behind the other species with greater size potential--the typical fish, male or female, is around 8.5 inches long, the weight about 3/4 pound. By year three, the males begin to outgrow the females, reaching around 10.9 inches versus 9.6 inches. The weight will be a bit over a pound for each.

Like other reef species, the black sea bass are protogynous hermaphrodites, with some of the females becoming males as they grow past age 3. A five-year-old male is likely to be around 14 inches long, while a female of this age is a couple inches shorter. For the few fish that reach age 10, length in males will approach 18 inches and weight around 4 1/2 pounds. Females are not known to exceed 17 inches at any age.

In areas where there are rock piles in deep creeks and bays, such as around Homosassa, Florida, spawning black sea bass sometimes push well up into areas that look more likely for redfish. Some of the creeks around Chassahowitzka Point have runs of humpbacks each spring, and to get to these holes the fish have to pass over at least a mile of knee-deep water before they reach the deeper pockets.

Except for these inshore excursions, larger sea bass stay at least four miles offshore in most areas, usually in water deeper than 8 feet. Finding them is a matter of fishing visible rockpiles, or of pulling a small spoon on a number 1 planer. In Florida's

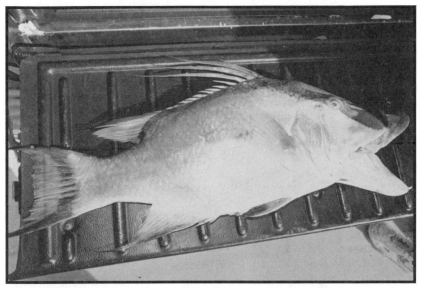

The hog snapper is actually a member of the wrasse family, but it's widely recognized as the best-tasting of all reef species. It's a tough fish to catch on hook-and-line, but live squid drifted over deep reefs sometimes connects

Big Bend area, there seems to be a shoreward push in late winter, a time when most other species can be hard to find, and sea bass chasers often catch more than a hundred fish in a morning when they locate the concentrations.

OTHER REEF SPECIES

The coney, *Epinephelus fulvus,* has white dots on an overall brown or red-gold body, plus blue-edged fins. There's also a brilliant yellow-gold phase. They're usually small, under 2 pounds, and most common in the Bahamas inshore reefs. Their tender flesh is super eating when you catch one large enough to clean-- they take both cut baits and small jigs readily.

The speckled hind, *Epinephelus drummondhayi*, is also known as the Kitty Mitchell, allegedly because Kitty, an historic waterfront lady of the night, had speckles on her . . . well, you get the idea.

The rust-colored body of this grouper is covered with small white dots, and the edges of the pelvic fins are yellow. Smaller fish may be overall gold with white spots. They get big, with the current record 42 pounds, 6 ounces caught off Destin, Fla. The usual grouper tactics will get them.

The red hind, *Epinephelus guttatus*, is one of the prettiest groupers. It has a gold/brown mottled body with bright red dots, which earn it the nickname strawberry grouper. It's common on reefs in the Keys and throughout the Bahamas, where it's readily caught on all types of cut bait. Maximum size is about 6 pounds, but the average fish is closer to a pound.

The white grunt, *Haemulon plumieri*, a.k.a. bluestripe grunt for the blue stripes on the head; main identifier, though, is the bright orange mouth. The general range is 20 to 100 feet over hard bottom. It grunts by grinding it's teeth, and the air bladder acts as an amplifier according to biologists. Grunts eat small reef species, crustaceans, etc. It's a common catch throughout Florida waters, and in the larger sizes is super table fare. Current IGFA record is 6 pounds, 8 ounces, taken off Georgia.

The lane snapper, *Lutjanus synagris*, is similar in body shape to the mangrove snapper but has a more reddish overall cast and pink and yellow lines on the side, sometimes a black spot under the dorsal fin. They're very aggressive and fun to catch on the holes in grass flats of the Florida Keys, where they'll take small plugs, jigs and bonefish flies. These inshore fish are rarely over 12 inches. On the reefs, however, the species sometimes exceeds 5 pounds. They can be caught with the same baits and tactics as mangrove snapper.

The yellowmouth grouper, *Mycteroperca interstitialis*, is tan with darker spots. The identifier is the bright yellow shading around the jaws and the eyes. Average fish is 3-4 pounds, but they reach at least 8 pounds. It's most common on deep ledges in South Florida. This is an aggressive grouper inclined to attack trolled lures as well as live baits.

11

ELECTRONICS FOR BOTTOM ANGLERS

Marine electronics are the eyes and ears of reef anglers, and without a good fish finder and position locator, successful bottom fishing is impossible. Fortunately, electronics have been getting better, smaller and cheaper each year, and presently it's possible to completely equip a reef rig with the basic necessities for little more than $1,000. Here's a look at some of the parameters you might consider when choosing your gear:

FISH FINDERS

Liquid Crystal Display (LCD) fish-finders or depth-sounders have pretty much taken over the market, displacing the popular paper "scratchers" that were dear to the heart of a generation of bottom-diggers. The LCD's require no paper changes, make no dust or noise, and have no moving parts to break down-- and they remain sealed water-tight, a major maintenance plus around saltwater. To be sure, some very serious anglers point out that LCD's even now don't offer the same degree of sharpness as a paper recorder, and don't offer a paper print-out that can be reviewed, marked up and kept for future reference. But the dependability, ease of use and low cost of LCD's have pretty much blown the paper charts out of the water, anyway, so we'll devote our attention to them, and to the next step up, Cathode

The well-equipped dash for a reef angler includes either loran or GPS plus a serious depthfinder. The old "scratcher" type is a favorite with long-time pros, but LCD and CRT machines are more trouble-free and just as effective.

Ray Tube sonar or CRT, which is technology much like what's found in your color television.

In selecting an LCD fish finder, consider the number of "pixels" you get in the vertical dimension first. These are the pencil-dots that make up an image in an LCD machine, and more is better. More pixels means a sharper image--although they also mean a higher price. Most quality machines also offer boat speed and water temperature readouts. Any serious bottom fisher will want both of these options so spring for the extra paddle-wheel and sensor.

When it comes to mounting your transducer, almost everybody puts them inside the hull these days. It's a clean installation, you don't see any wires or parts, and there's nothing to get snagged by a Magnum Rapala. However, shooting through an inch of fiberglass is bound to degrade the signal from even the best depthfinders. If you want the very best results from your depthfinder, it's better to get the transducer into direct contact with the water.

You can do this by hanging it off the transom, which is easy but not pretty because you have the cable running over the transom, with the transducer mounted in a pop-up bracket screwed to the transom itself. You have to be careful to get it in the right spot so there's no turbulence coming out from under the hull, or readings will be distorted. (Try to mount it between strakes, where the water flow is likely to be "cleaner", but don't put it in the path of the prop, about 7 inches either side of the centerline, because this will interfere with the efficiency of your propulsion system.) The transom mount is the best solution in aluminum boats, where getting a good seal on through-hull fittings can be difficult, and where shooting through the hull is impossible due to interference from the metal.

The second approach is to cut a hole in the bottom of the boat (gulp!) and secure the transducer in the hole. Thru-hulls come with mechanical sealing systems, but if you goof, your boat sinks. Obviously, this is not a good first-project for amateur electronics installers. And, on most installations, the transducer sticks out below the bottom of the boat where it's subject to damage from floating debris or from trailering.

The best installation is via a built-in pod, like those used in Hydra-Sports and some other hulls. The transducer fits into the pod, with the face perfectly flush with the running surface of the boat, while the cable runs through a glassed-in and completely water-tight fitting up inside the pod. This gives great clarity and no interference with the water flow, plus the transducer is protected from damage.

LCD fish finders offer ease of operation and a sharp picture of bottom. Some like this Eagle Ultra III are also completely water-tight.

For fishing out to 50 feet, wide-beam machines are probably best because they allow adequate bottom coverage over the short distance to the bottom. But in deep water, over 100 feet, you might prefer a narrow beam or a dual beam unit that can be switched back and forth, because a broad-beam shows you too much--you can't tell when you're directly over the fish. The broad beam helps you find the reef, but the narrow beam keeps you on the exact spot.

Which brand to buy? All the major makes including Lowrance, Techsonic, Si-Tex, Apelco and others are fine. Choose one that speaks to you as an easy, intuitive machine to use. The only way to go wrong is to buy from a new company--a lot of them come and go, leaving you with a machine that can't be repaired due to a lack of parts.

CRT machines do all the things that LCD's do, but they do it in color. Thus, bottom may be red, baitfish blue and grouper yellow. The readouts are much more vivid and bright, and for those who can afford it and have the extra space required, these machines are definitely the way to go. However, full-featured killer machines like those from Furuno and Raytheon start at about $2500 and go up, fast.

LORAN VS GPS

Is GPS superior to loran? It has the potential to be so--as all who watched pictures of the Iraq war will remember, GPS is capable of pinpoint navigation to a square the size of a chimney from a distance of several hundred miles. But presently, in a Rube Goldberg system, the military requires the signals to be "dithered" or degraded, introducing inaccuracy into the most accurate navigation system in history. The logic of this is that the dithering will prevent the bad guys from using our own GPS satellites to home in on U.S. installations with missiles. If you don't have the proper decodifier, you can't get the accuracy--but you can still land your missile within 100 yards of where you want it! A hundred yards won't make any difference at all if the nukes ever start to fly, though that could matter a lot in a terrorist situation with a single conventional warhead aimed at the White House.

Anyway, we live in dangerous times, so the feds are putting up a series of towers that will fix the messed up signals and make them accurate again, introducing a differential that corrects the error they put in with dithering. Why, you might ask, won't a terrorist buy a differential GPS and mount it on his missile? Or if they're doing this so they can just turn off the towers in time of war, why not just introduce the dither in time of war? Don't ask, these are your federal tax dollars at work and you have no right to try to control their use.

Anyway, GPS works pretty good despite the efforts to make it fail, and once you get a lock on a spot with a given machine, you can dependably go back there to within a hundred feet or so, which is about as good as most lorans can manage. They're going to phase out the loran system eventually anyway, so I guess we might as well get used to it. And with the prices of GPS falling below $500 as this is written, they're actually cheaper by half than full-featured lorans used to be. And the little handheld models make it possible for you to transfer your navigation system from one boat to another--some are so small they fit in your shirt pocket, and hooked up to the 12-volt system in any boat via a cigarette-lighter plug, they can have you navigating electronically in a jon boat.

What type of unit should you buy? If you like things simple and/or don't have a lot of space in your radio box, an "all-in-one" system like the Lowrance 350A is a winner. You get GPS, plotter, digital speedometer, water temperature gauge and a full-feature LCD depthfinder in a box about half the size of a loaf of bread.

No matter which machine you choose, put it where you can see it easily. Don't make the mistake of putting your fish finder in the overhead radio box, as I did when rigging out my first grouper boat. While it's nice to have everything up there out of the way and in a locking box, you have to tilt your head back and look up to find your spot, and in a long day of fishing you'll develop a major crick in your neck from that viewing angle.

The navigation system can be up there, because you don't have to watch it all that closely after you punch in your destination, but you don't want that fish finder much out of the line of sight--it should go on the dash, just low enough so it doesn't restrict your view ahead of the boat. Unfortunately, most boats don't have a radio box in the right position, so you have to put the finder on top of the dash and then unhook it for safe overnight storage.

BOOK OF NUMBERS

In any case, those who use either loran or GPS can benefit from the latest edition of "Coastal Loran & GPS Coordinates" by Captain Rod and Susie Stebbins.

The authors are from Tampa, and the book is heavy on reefs and wrecks along the Gulf Coast. More than 70 wrecks from Manatee, Hillsborough, Pinellas and Pasco counties alone are

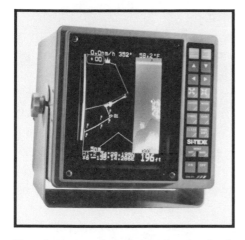

CRT machines like this SI-TEX give a full-color picture of structure, bait and fish. Unit shown includes the popular Global Positioning Satellite capabilities.

listed. In total, it includes both the lat/lon and TD numbers for some 8,500 spots, covering nearly all the coastal states. The 220-page book is the result of some 13 years of charting and diving by the Stebbinses, as well as from input by teams of hired coordinate-seekers who send in locations from distant waters.

The book is valuable for the waypoints alone, but for those just getting into electronic navigation, the first 40 pages of in-depth information on how to use and fine-tune loran and GPS are just what's needed for a solid grounding in the art.

Rod Stebbins says he wore out eight boats in putting together all the locations. Given that, the $33 cover price is not excessive. Make checks to Weak Industries, and mail to AuCoin & Associates, 1355 Snell Isle Blvd. NE, St. Petersburg, FL 33704.

GOT YOUR EARS ON?

VHF radio is a must for all boats used for offshore operations--it's your safety-line when things go badly wrong. And it's also very useful if you need a little help in finding the fish.

Nearly all 25-watt VHF radios made by well-known manufacturers will do the job. The main difference between good and poor performance is usually in the antenna or ''whip''. A

6- to 9-foot antenna with lots of power does the job. A little 18-inch wire whip is fine for a flats boat that never gets more than five miles from help, but when you're out there 20 miles, you want some reach.

It's a good idea to opt for a waterproof radio. Humminbird and others make them so tight they can be operated underwater. While your radio won't get this wet in normal use, the waterproofing helps keep out salt mist than invades every nook and cranny of a boat used around the coast. Other things being equal, a water-tight system will outlive one that's not just because there's no NaCl inside the connections.

Handheld VHF radios are useful inshore or when you get within a few miles of another boat, but these 5 watt units just don't have the punch to work effectively offshore. A better backup is cellular phone, at least in most areas where you can hook up with a roamer. Just be aware that no cell phone is waterproof--keep them sealed in plastic bags until needed. And shut off that damned thing from incoming calls--I don't want to hear it just when the bite starts!

12

THE ART OF ANCHORING

One of the toughest parts of successful groupering is learning to anchor just right, so that the stern of the boat is precisely positioned over the fish on those numbers you have cadged. If the anchor doesn't hold, or if you're off by 20 feet, you might as well be a mile away, because grouper are not out prospecting for hooks. If you don't drop it right on their dinner table, you can forget it.

GROUND TACKLE

First, you have to have the correct "ground tackle" as the old salts call it--the right anchor and line to handle your boat. Only serious anchors of the fluke or plow style are appropriate for offshore work, of course--mushroom styles and others just don't have the holding power/weight ratio needed. To be sure, a 55-gallon oil drum filled with cement would hold you in any weather, but there might be some complaints from the crewman assigned to bring it back aboard.

The right size fluke anchor is about a pound per foot--that is, you need a 20-pounder for a 20-foot boat, 25 pounds for 25 feet, etc, though you can get by with a little less in moderate weather. Add to it at least 10 feet of 3/8 galvanized chain--that's right, chain big enough to hold a medium-sized banana trader. You want this stuff not for strength, but for weight--it slinks on the bottom and lowers the angle of pull on the anchor shank, which greatly improves holding power. It also protects the anchor rode or rope from coral. Hitch it up with the appropriate galvanized clevis, pinned in place.

The anchor line should be fat, both for strength and so you can handle it easily. Don't consider anything less than 5/8" nylon for offshore work. It's easier on the hands than smaller diameters, has the strength needed to extract an anchor stuck on a rock, and doesn't tangle as readily as smaller stuff. On the other hand, it's expensive and takes lots of storage space. (If your boat doesn't have a suitable anchor locker, make use of a large clothes basket bolted down on the bow. This keeps the line under control and the crate-style construction lets it dry rapidly.)

Anchor floats are a big plus for those who raise and lower the anchor dozens of times a day, as most successful reef anglers do. The float, an orange plastic ball about the size of a beach ball, is hooked to a stainless steel ring with an open loop on one side. To raise the anchor, you slip the line through the loop, drop the float overboard and motor ahead. The line slides through the loop until it's directly over the anchor, jerks it out of the bottom, and then sweeps it to the surface. All you have to do is pull in the line and the float, much easier than hauling all that dead weight from the bottom.

A capstan is also useful for bottom bumpers. It's less costly than a complete electric anchor winch system, but works just as slick. You simply toss a loop over it when you want to raise anchor, hit the button and pull on the line, and up comes the anchor as fast as you can hand-over-hand.

THE ART OF ANCHORING

The art of anchoring is realizing that you have to get a looong way upstream in order to have the boat settle on your alleged hotspot. First, the basic seamanship 101 review: Scope is the ratio of anchor line to water depth. Just to keep the boat in place,

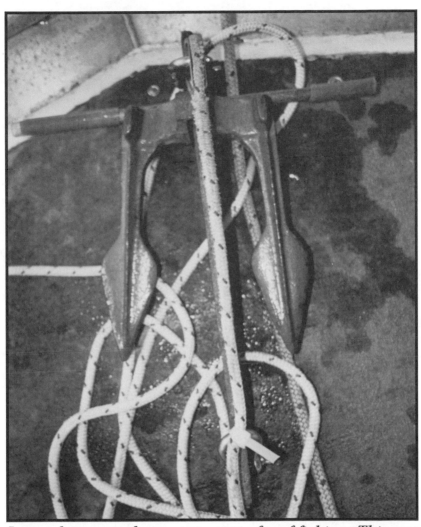

Large, heavy anchors are a part of reef fishing. This one is rigged with a break-away device that allows the hook to be pulled from the bottom if it should snag in a rock.

you need a scope of at least 3:1, remember, and in more wind or waves, you need 5:1 or more.

So, if you find fish in 60 feet of water, you've got to drop 180 feet of line just to hold position. How far up-current do you have to travel to achieve that scope? Based on the old right triangle formula, $a^2 + b^2 = c^2$, it's about 170 feet. But in fact, it makes better sense to go a lot farther, maybe 200 to 250 feet up-current before you lower away. This allows you time and space to get the anchor firmly set, then back down on your spot by letting out more line. (If you're fishing a spot that you know well or in water shallow and clear enough to see the reef, it's best to anchor uptide without running the boat directly over the numbers--that way, the fish won't be put on the alert.)

Cleat off at the upstream edge of the rock or structure first. That way, there's less chance of spooking fish with the mass and noise from the boat, and you also get the benefit of the scent of your baits wafting down over the whole feeding area with the flow. After you work the edge for a while, you let out another 10 feet and work that area, and then another 10 feet until you've covered the entire spot.

Of course, days when you hang straight downstream from the anchor are not all that common--the boat always wanders around like a kite at the end of a string, and this is more pronounced with more rope out. One way to control it, if there's lots of tide running, is to turn the wheel and cause the lower units of your outboards to act as rudders. The force of the tide against them will push the boat in the direction you want.

You can also "sail" the boat to one side or the other by moving the line to a breast cleat about half-way back on the forward gunnels. Cleat it on the port gunnel and you sail to starboard, and vice-versa. How far? Not very, but as Captain Dave Zalewski of Clearwater, Fla., says, finding grouper is a game of inches--a move of just a couple yards to one side may put your baits on the motherlode.

Most grouper anglers don't use stern anchors because they don't want an extra rope over the side where they'll hopefully be wrestling up big fish. But there are times when a small deadweight anchor lowered straight down from the back cleat can keep you on the spot a lot better--and if you attach a block of chum to it before lowering, you may stir up the fish below, too.

FINDING THE HONEY HOLE

Even when everything goes right, it often takes a bit of thought to get exactly on the spot where the fish are holding. It helps to visualize yourself standing on top of a 100-foot-tall building, trying to drop the bait into a garbage can on the street, with a strong side-wind blowing.

If the reef is 100 yards long and 20 yards wide, you have more options than you want. Fish can be anywhere along it, and when the boat sets up over the rocks, they may move out from the prime holding spot to secondary hideouts. This is not a problem on small, isolated rocks where the fish don't have anywhere else to go, but the bigger the reef, the more likely it is that you'll have a problem setting up over just the right spot, even with the help of your depthfinder.

Of course, those adept at casting with heavy gear can probe in all directions, but this strategy often results in at least as many snags as fish. When you try to pull a weighted hook sideways across a reef, it rarely avoids catching Mother Earth. With modest weights and active live baits like pinfish or grunts, you can often get away with it long enough to get bit, though, and sometimes these tosses into undisturbed waters result in the largest fish of the trip.

The other alternative is to re-anchor, which becomes progressively less fun as you fish deeper and deeper water. Wise sailing skippers have long known the value of "deck apes", brawny young guys who will crank on winches in return for a day on the water, and it's wise for graying grouper captains to cultivate the fishing habits of some similarly muscular dudes to be anchorman. (We are, of course, gender-neutral on this topic, and any well-conditioned young women who wish to pull the anchor are also welcome aboard at any time.)

Whoever handles the tug of war with Mr. Danforth, the idea is to simply get the hook up off the bottom 10 feet, ease the bow right or left a boat-length or two, and let it go again. You then work out the line length progressively as above. Eventually, you fish the entire rockpile this way, showing your bait to all the fish present.

Of course, this tactic could kill a reef in the days before the current size and bag limits because covering all the water around a particular number raised the possibility of wiping out most of the fish population. But with the current rules, it makes sense to probe all of the available habitat, keeping those you want for the freezer, releasing the rest to re-supply your honey hole. One tip from old grouper skippers, though: if you're on a number that's exclusively yours, it's wise to put back a couple of the big fish as well as the shorts. Big fish attract big fish, and if you don't want to wait years for your secret spot to produce more big ones, it's best to leave some "seed" adults in place to act as decoys.

13

TROLLING TACTICS

Finding the fish is 90 percent of the battle in bottom fishing, and one of the best ways to sort out the hotspots is by trolling. At 4 to 6 knots, you can cover hundreds of likely locations in a few hours and you have lures in the water continuously. Trolling is less labor-intensive than raising and lowering the anchor dozens of times, as you must do when you're searching for fish in a new area.

And there are times when it's not only the best locator tactic but also the best production method--the more active grouper like gags and blacks, in particular, love a moving target.

WHERE TO TROLL

Trolling works best in water less than 100 feet deep. After that, the logistics of handling lure, downrigger and tackle make it a toss-up with run-and-gun bottom fishing.

In general, you don't want to start trolling until you're in the "red zone", the area where the combination of bottom structure, water temperature and season should combine to produce a high probability of success. Random trolling without first getting basic information on large patterns of rock structure in your fishing area is rarely productive.

One of the better aids to this research is the series of offshore charts produced by International Sailing Supply, 320 Cross

Street, Punta Gorda, FL 33950-9972. These waterproof charts have all the general navigational information of standard NOAA charts, but in addition include marked locations of rocks, wrecks, artificial reefs and other fish attractors, complete with GPS coordinates. It's wise to carry one along and use it to put you in the general area where locals are catching fish. Then, as you begin to locate your own hotspots, you can mark them on the chart and soon develop an easily visualized trolling pattern. It's a lot more evident this way than if you simply write disconnected numbers in a little black book or punch them into the memory of your GPS.

TROLLING SHIP CHANNELS

While a three-foot break a couple hundred yards long is considered a rare find by grouper-diggers in the open Gulf, within Florida's major harbors there are endless miles of breaks with relief often exceeding 20 feet! These are made up of the sides of the shipping channels that have been dredged through the bays and inshore waters, and nearly all of them are loaded with grouper.

Tampa Bay is a case in point. The main shipping channels here average around 45 feet deep, through the bay bottom where average depth ranges from 22 to 25 feet.

Vance Tice, a jig-maker in Tampa, has perfected a technique for working this drop that consistently turns out lots of gag grouper, even when Gulf anglers are finding fish scarce.

RIGGER TACTICS

Tice uses downriggers to present his baits along the edge. Dropping his 8-inch-long "Bubba" jig tails to bottom on 3- to 4-ounce heads with the help of 10-pound rigger weights, he keeps the lures constantly in the strike zone, and the results are usually grouper fingers for dinner.

He uses the fin-type riggers, which he says track better than round balls and also create less disturbance in the water. And he runs the jigs a full 100 feet behind the rigger weight, attaching

108

Vance Tice of Bubba Jigs finds lots of gags in the ship channels of Tampa Bay. He pulls his lures a full 100 feet behind the downrigger ball.

the line with a heavy rubber band wrapped around the mono, then to a snap-hook. When the jig bumps bottom the rubber band stretches and springs it loose most of the time, but when a fish latches on the band breaks and frees the line. It's a better system than standard rigger clips for this bottom-trolling, because most spring free too easily when the lure hits a rock. The band winds easily through the rod guides, allowing an easy retrieve of the long drop-back line when a fish is brought to the boat.

One angler has to man the wheel, keeping a sharp eye on the depthfinder to follow the ins and outs of the channel. Though the marker buoys make the channel appear to be fairly straight, in fact the wall zigs and zags by 30 feet in many areas, and if the boat doesn't turn everytime there's a jut, the jigs snag. The lures have to pass close to the wall, though, or the grouper won't swim out to get the bait--maybe because visibility is frequently poor due to frequent passage of ships, which stir up the bottom mud.

Setting the rigger to the right depth takes a bit of practice. Though most downriggers have depth meters, the meter only measures how much cable is put out, not the actual depth at which the weight is running. All weights "kite" or sweep upward due to the movement of the boat through the current. Tice says that in 42 feet, he usually lets out about 55 feet of cable to put the lures within a couple feet of bottom.

"With jigs on long drop-backs, the jigs actually run two to four feet below the ball," says Tice. "If there's no current or you're trolling with the current, the jig will run four feet deeper. If there's lots of current and you're going against it, the jig may only drop a foot or two. So you have to keep an eye on how the lures run and if you're getting snagged a lot, shorten up the rigger cable. If you're going over fish that mark on the LCD and not getting hits, drop the weight down farther."

Tice also notes that the fish usually strike best when the lure is trolled with the current, since fish tend to face into the flow to watch for baitfish traveling in and out with the tides. However, he says some of his largest fish have been caught trolling against the tide, so it pays to work both ways.

SPEED CHECK

Tom Tomanini, a Bay area guide who's also a pro at trolling for the grouper, takes a more intuitive approach, whether trolling channels or open-sea reefs.

"I usually drop the ball until it hits bottom, then crank it up three turns," he says. "If the lures snag, I crank it up another turn."

Tomanini also points out that boat speed has a major influence on how the lures run.

"At 1000 rpms, the lures might be right down there at 42 feet, and if you speed up to 1500 they may be 8 feet off the bottom. On the other hand, when you make a turn, the jigs are going to fall toward bottom, so you need to apply more power until you're completely straightened out."

He also says that anglers should consider the effect of wind on their boats. Downwind legs will be faster and the lures run

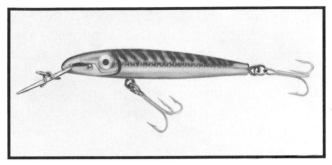

The 112MR MirrOlure is often a very productive lure to use for trolling behind a downrigger ball.

higher than on upwind legs, if you maintain the same rpms. So making use of a paddlewheel or GPS speed indicator can help you adjust to keep up the best speed, usually around 4 knots.

Tice likes chartreuse or hot pink tails, and says there are definite preferences varying with the seasons.

"It's not consistent, but we usually put one color on each rod, and if one starts catching all the fish, we go with that color on both."

Other lures that work well when trolled behind a downrigger ball include six-inch chrome spoons like the Accetta and Captain Action, plus large diving plugs including the Magnum Rapala, MirrOlure 113 and jumbo Bomber. An advantage of these latter lures is that they float at rest, so when you stop to reel in a fish, the other lures don't sink to bottom and snag. Just be sure to use plugs with oversized, 3X-strong hooks, because the surge of a 20-pound gag on 50-pound tackle will straighten lesser hardware.

Standard tackle for all these baits is 50-pound-test line on Penn Senator[R] 113 HLW reels and very stout, 6- to 7-foot trolling rods.

With Tomanani's Dorado 22, which has a 200-Merc mounted on a bracket, the anglers use 4' booms on the Penn FathomMaster[R] 600 downriggers. This helps keep the cables clear of the outboard on turns. With transom mount outboards or inboards, Tice says, a 2-foot boom is adequate and makes it easier to tend the baits.

111

With either boom, one thing you learn very quickly is that you NEVER back up when a cable is down--otherwise, you immediately cut off your $15 weight, and often have to pick the wire out of the prop as well.

A GPS system can be useful in marking particularly productive rocks, as well is in plotting the trolling course, allowing you to return over the exact course as often as you like. In general, though, you can pretty well locate your spots because there's a buoy every half-mile, often much closer. As you'd expect, areas that have more cluttered or rocky bottom often hold fish best. However, when trolling with downriggers, Tice advises staying clear of areas with lots of irregular bottom because this always results in snags.

"There are a lot of fish in the rougher areas, but you can't troll them," he says. "It's best to go in and drift those spots"

DRIFTING A JIG

To drift, he changes to monster jig-heads, 8 to 12 ounces. These are usually dressed with bucktail, and with the 8-inch chartreuse swimmer tail.

It's easy fishing--all you do is drop the weight until it hits bottom, then leave it there, raising up now and then to make sure there's no debris.

"Don't jig it," advises Tice. "The tail is swimming and the bucktail puffs every time the boat rocks--that's all the action you need. If you jig a lot, you get slack and can't feel when you get a strike. If you leave it down there, you've got tight line and you're ready to set."

He said that the very heavy jigs are essential because they stay in contact with the bottom and don't kite. Even 4 to 6 ounce jigs are too light in 40-foot-depths, he says. And if there's a fast drift, you may have to feed line even with the heavy jigs to keep the bait in contact with the structure. It's the exact opposite of inshore fishing, where a lighter jig and a slower fall is often the

112

The downrigger allows precise depth control, a critical factor in successful trolling for grouper. A long boom on the rigger helps the cable to clear outboards rigged on a bracket.

key to getting more strikes--here, you want the heaviest possible jig and the fastest fall so that you maintain bottom contact.

DOWNRIGGER GEAR

Basic manual downriggers suitable for reef species can be purchased for about $200 for the 24-inch boom, $250 for the 48-inch boom. Electric models which automatically retrieve the weights are very handy, and go for about $350 to $450. Some have programs which will raise and lower the lures a specified amount while you troll, which seems to turn on fish at times when a straight pull does not.

Lead balls and other weights range from $15 to $30. Another tack is to replace the weight with a downrigger planer like the Z-Wing, which weighs very little and is easy to raise when tripped, but which has almost no "kite" or blowback due to the design.

If you put out 50 feet of cable, the baits are running at 50 feet--it's a good system. There are two models, one for 6 knots or less, one for higher speeds--each is about $40.

A useful extra for any downrigger is a rod-holder mount, which allows simply dropping the mount and the rigger into the trolling holder on your gunnel. Otherwise, you have to dog it down with wing nuts each time you want to use the riggers. The mounts are about $50.

PLANERS

Trip-style planers are designed to get your lure deep without the expense and the extra work involved with a downrigger. A flat metal plate acts as a diving lip to force the planer down, but when a fish hits it trips the plate upward, allowing you to reel in without fighting the pull of the planer. The smaller models can be attached direct to your fishing line, which makes handling very easy. They are rated for the depth they run, with the smallest running shallower, the largest running deeper. A size 1 goes to about 10 feet, size 2 to 20 feet and so on up through size 6, which runs 60 feet. Sizes up through 3 can be attached direct, while the larger ones have to be run on a separate cable, so don't offer any advantage over the downriggers.

Many anglers replace the wire cable on their riggers with 125-pound-test mono, which has about the same breaking strength as the braided cable but doesn't "hum" as it comes through the water. It's not clear whether the metallic vibration annoys fish--probably not much, with the lure 100 feet back from the weight--but it assuredly annoys fishermen who stand close to it.

Put together the right gear with a systematic trolling pattern over likely bottom areas and you can find fish anywhere your travels take you.

14

LIVE BAITS FOR LUNKERS

There's no question that live baits are the best bet for big grouper and snapper. Cut baits will usually do the job when you can't get livies, but compare the catches of those who use live bait versus cut bait and the advantages of providing a wiggling, flashing target are obvious.

One major advantage of the live bait is that it's too big for the "junk" fish to attack. While they may steal four out of five drops with cut bait or dead whole baits like cigar minnows or sardines, they can't down a live pinfish. So the bait stays down there long enough for Mr. Big to swim over, investigate, and chow down. It gives you a tremendous increase in bottom time over a day of fishing, and that results in more keepers in the box.

On the downside, you have to go to some trouble and invest some time to find and catch most types of live bait--few bait shops keep baits of the type to interest the offshore species.

SCALED SARDINES

On the eastern Gulf Coast, probably the most effective of all live baits is the scaled sardine. They're durable, very active on the hook, and absolute ice cream to every species of grouper and snapper. The only problem is, there are a limited number of areas where sardines are easy to find, and these days there

Scaled sardines are a favorite bait of inshore grouper and snapper anglers. The baits make good live chum over shallow rocks, too.

are lots of boats after them because inshore anglers like to fish sardines just as well as offshore anglers do. If you plan on catching your grouper bait at one of the outside markers, you'd better get up early, leave the dock before dawn, and be the first boat there. While sardines are prolific and very fast-growing, the areas where anglers can find and catch them best, over grassy shallows covered with clear water, are limited. And some seem to be reaching their limits in terms of castnetting pressure.

"It's harder to catch the bait than the fish some days," says Captain Rob McCue of New Port Richey. "You may have to run 10 miles out of the way to get your sardines. Sometimes you spend two hours catching bait."

LOCATING SARDINES

The places where most fishermen find their baits are natural sardine attractors. The baitfish like to roam the inner edges of open water, and often move in from these areas to the first turtle grass flat at the edge of deep water. They're commonly found on the first grassy area inside a pass, as well.

The largest sardines--the best grouper baits--often hang around channel markers and range markers in water 8 to 15 feet deep. Rock piles in water 3 to 10 feet deep also sometimes hold pods of sardines, as do piers and other structures that give them some protection from predators.

There are also plenty of scaled sardines in the larger open bays and in the Gulf itself, but finding these fish is a problem since the points of concentration change continuously. And, catching them in the deeper water is difficult because successful castnetting usually depends on trapping the fish against bottom.

The trick, says McCue, is to find inshore areas that other anglers overlook. Sometimes a scattering of rocks miles from any landmark can be a honeyhole. A fallen marker, a boat wreck, or debris from an old stilt house can also be keys to finding them.

"It takes a lot of running and looking, but once you have two or three of these spots, it's money in the bank so long as nobody else finds them," he says.

FATAL ATTRACTION

Once you sight bait--usually by noting their flashing forms and the ripple they make at the surface as they feed--bringing them into castnet range is the next job.

While unmolested bait usually comes quickly to the slightest hint of a chum made from whole wheat bread and canned sardines, the baits are much harder to lure in areas where they are netted frequently.

McCue likes to set up well uptide of whatever structure is holding the baits and lure them to him with chum, rather than anchoring right on the spot and possibly pushing the baits off.

His chum starts with the standard bread/sardine mix, but he adds a major helping of menhaden oil to the smelly mess as well.

The pungent brown oil is available at baitshops that cater to offshore fishermen.

"The oil makes a slick that spreads out for hundreds of yards," says McCue. "It really seems to have a special appeal for sardines. They'll come to it when they completely ignore the standard chum."

Some anglers also like to add anise oil and canned jack mackerel to the chum mix. Whatever the mixture, it's dribbled overboard in dime-sized droplets, just enough to create a scent trail that will bring the bait within castnet range, about 10 feet from the boat.

When there are plenty of baits within range, McCue tosses out a "bomb" of chum, a whole handful, which immediately sends the baitfish into a tight swarm as they attack the food. Then it's time to toss the net.

NET RESULTS

Most castnet pros like a net with a nominal measure of 10 to 12 feet. These nets open to a circle about double their nominal size, so cover a lot of water.

"You have to have a big net and one with lots of belly and lots of lead," says McCue. "A flat net, one that's built with a minimum of webbing in it to keep down cost, won't open right and won't settle over the baits the way it should."

He says that the lead weights on the net should total 15 pounds or more, so that they quickly pull the net to bottom, keeping the sardines from swimming out underneath.

His other advice is to make the first throw count.

"You always catch the most on the first throw, because they're not spooked then. If you make a bad throw, you're going to have a tough time getting those baits back in close."

THREAD HERRING AND MENHADEN

Threadfins, known as "greenbacks" in many areas, don't stay alive in the well nearly as well as sardines, but they are more

Sardines, threadfins and menhaden are all best caught in a large, heavily-weighted castnet. Most serious live-baiters prefer a 12-foot net with about 15 pounds of weight.

abundant in many areas. They don't come to chum, but it's usually possible to catch adequate numbers by working around the beaches in water 8 to 20 feet deep early in the day. The fish are often on top, which makes location easy because you simply ease up to the "bait ripple" and toss the net.

Menhaden reach larger sizes than threads, but otherwise are generally found in similar areas. They show a particular preference for outflow areas near inlets, where they find nutrient-rich water and abundant food. Like threads, they often create a ripple on the surface.

However, in hard-fished areas, it's often necessary to find either of these baits by watching the depthfinder over deeper water. When a ball of bait is spotted, the throw is made off the stern and the boat jammed into reverse so that the net has slack

These live bait rigs often jerk up half-a-dozen blue runners and pinfish on a drop. The string of number 10 hooks needs no bait.

on the brailles to sink. This takes a heavy net (at least 15 pounds on the leads) and teamwork, but it's effective.

PINFISH

There are few baits more appealing to a big gag than a lively pinfish, and these prickly critters are abundant and easy to catch anywhere there's grassy bottom. Along the northwest coast of Florida the pins are known as "shiners" for their flashing sides as they feed by the thousands in water 3 to 8 feet deep. In these areas, tossing a handful of chum quickly brings in all you want to the cast net. However, these tend to be small--if you want larger pins for bigger fish, you may have to hook-and-line them around markers and rocks.

Use a light spinning rig or cane pole and 6-pound-test mono, rigged with a bait-getter string of number 10 hooks. You can

Live squirrelfish are a prime bait for large gags and red grouper. They survive well in a livewell and on the hook.

sweeten the hooks with bits of shrimp or bacon rind to make things happen fast.

Pinfish are among the most durable of baits, able to live several days in a live well and still be active on the hook. And for anglers fishing deeper than 100 feet, they're the bait of choice because they have an uncanny ability to survive the rocket-sled ride to bottom without being crushed by the rapid pressure change. Delicate baits like sardines don't handle this well, so are best reserved for shallower water when fished live.

OTHER SPECIES

Sand perch, better-known as squirrelfish, are a favorite of most grouper. They're commonly caught on the sand patches between the reefs, usually with a bit of shrimp on a string of number 8 hooks.

Just about any small reef species can be fodder for grouper and snapper--pigfish, croakers, sailors choice and grunts are all excellent. And for big grouper, a live blue runner or "hardtail" 8 to 10 inches long is hard to beat. All of these can be caught on bits of squid on small hooks. On the southeast shore of Florida, a live goggle-eye is a great bait for whopper gags and blacks, and might also lure up a sailfish, as well--they're caught by trolling tiny jigs along the beach reefs at dawn and dusk, or you can buy them from live-bait boats at the major marinas--for as much as $120 per dozen during the winter sailfish runs!

Ballyhoo also make excellent live baits, and they're abundant enough along the southeast coast of Florida to be readily netted. They're also super when used dead as tippers for a big jig, and this offering bounced along the deep ledges is murder on big blacks. Anglers in south Florida like to make a ballyhoo "plug" by cutting off the head and tail and rigging the resultant chunk on a short-shank 5/0 hook. It's a durable bait and just the right size for a grouper or snapper to inhale whole.

LIVELY LIVEWELLS

Because live bait can be hard to come by, it makes sense to equip your boat with a livewell that will keep what you're able to catch healthy all day long. That means a rounded well that holds at least 40 gallons, with a powerful pump supplying a continuous flow of fresh sea water. Many experts add a bubbler or aerator to put additional oxygen in the water, as well.

Of course, even when bait dies it can continue to be an excellent offering for most types of bottom fish. And for those not used, many anglers take home their casualties and freeze them as dead bait for future trips, particularly in winter when fresh bait becomes scarce. The dead leftovers can also be ground up and frozen as chum.

THEY COME TO CHUM

Live baits, cut baits and artificials are all more effective if you fish them in areas where chum has the fish in a biting mood. Best chum is fresh-ground fish, and some anglers use 12-volt meat grinders to convert bait to fishburger on the water. Threadfins and menhaden are among the best species for this, but any fish will do.

Chumming shallow reefs in water no deeper than 20 feet, simply letting the mix dribble on the surface and drift down will do the job of waking up the fish and pulling them to the boat. In deeper water, though, some special tactics may be needed to get the chum down to where the fish are before the current carries it off.

In areas where there are not a lot of sharks, a weighted mesh bag on a nylon cord will put the gurry down to the level of the reef. Some guys attach this to their anchor chain, which puts the scent upcurrent of the boat and draws the fish right through the baits as they pursue the trail.

Where sharks are abundant, you may want to use a 4" PVC pipe about 18" long, with caps on each end and 1/2" holes drilled throughout to sink the chum. Use a 10' length of aircraft cable as leader to protect against sharks biting off your canister.

Yellowtail fishermen often make "sandballs" with glass minnow chum, mixing the tiny baitfish (available frozen in bait shops in the Florida Keys) with beach mud to make a dense mix that goes deep.

One big advantage of chum is that you can sometimes move the fish a considerable distance from the rocks, and this gives a better chance of landing hooked lunkers. Always start chumming well away from the reef, moving in close only after the fish quit coming out to meet you.

15

HAPPY HOOKING

You have to hook 'em before you can cook 'em, and hooking them can sometimes be a bit of a trick. In most fishing for the reef species, you're fishing vertically instead of horizontally, and the changeover takes some practice for those who cut their angling teeth on the inshore species.

A vertical drop of 60 to 200 feet means there's usually a major belly in the line due to current and the swing of the boat at anchor, and this makes it difficult to tell when you've got a bite. And, getting that bow out of the line, which has to be done before the hook moves at all, takes a major effort.

LEVER ACTION
Here's the tactic that works best according to top grouper diggers like Captain Dave Markett of Tampa, a noted flats guide who used to make a major part of his income by commercial fishing grouper--he's one of the best ''hookers'' I've ever fished with: Markett uses his left hand as a fulcrum on the foregrip of the rod. His right hand goes on the back end of the main grip, and he fishes with the rod tip down, almost touching the water.

When he feels a bite, he levers down on the right hand, up on the left, which whips the rod tip upward with tremendous speed. This sweeps up any slack and snaps the hook home. It works much better than holding the rod around the reel area and trying to snatch it upward with both hands, which is the natural instinct of anglers used to using plug-casting gear inshore. And because there's so much travel of the rod tip, all slack is swept up, giving a tight line and a hard hook-set.

Knowing when to strike is another matter, of course. With live bait, you'll often feel the bait get nervous, transmitted by small twitches of the line, as a fish approaches. Then there's a bump as the bait is inhaled, the grouper or snapper sucking it in by vacuuming water through its mouth and out the gills. That's the time to set the hook.

Often with gags, they'll "freight-train" the bait, attacking at full speed and just about jerking you to your knees, so there's no question that they've got it. This is the best time to strike, and with live bait it usually results in a hookup.

NOW WHO'S THE JERK?

Cut bait presents another problem. You often get a bump as the fish tastes or bats at the bait but doesn't take it fully into the mouth. And sometimes the little guys come in tap-tap-tapping while the big boy holds back, deciding whether to attack. If you strike at that point, you jerk the bait away from the larger fish. So with cut bait, you have to wait for a more authoritative pull on the line.

Some anglers keep enough tension to hold the bait just off bottom a foot or two, and strike when there's a feeling of a slight heaviness or increase in weight. It takes almost a sixth sense to fish this way, but good anglers load up with the tactic while the next guy at the rail keeps reeling up a bare hook. (Some charter skippers advise anglers new to bottom fishing to simply start reeling when they feel weight, and forget all about setting the hook. This only works with fresh, tough baits that the fish can't readily knock off the hook, though.)

126

Eric Coppin of Weeki Wachee shows how it's done. Coppin is a believer in keeping the rod high and cranking hard during the first moments after hook-up to a heavy fish.

Hooking snapper is even more challenging because they attack quickly, pop the bait off the hook and leave you striking water. Lighter rods like the Penn 3145ARW or the SBG-6760 stand-up spinning rod give an advantage here--you have to feel the slightest bite, and you need all the speed you can get in the hookset.

The new high-tech braided lines, without the stretch of mono, also give an advantage. These lines are almost like fishing with wire cable, and when you move the rod tip an inch, the hook also moves an inch--it's a huge plus in hook-setting. (Penn warns that it's possible to ''overload'' a rod with these lines because the small diameter encourages anglers to spool up with 80-pound

This is a true test of tackle. When a 20-pounder heads for the rocks, it's no time for mercy on gear or fish.

on tackle designed for 40-pound-test mono. If the drag is locked down tight, even top quality rods can be destroyed.)

PLAYING THE FISH

In a word, don't.

Once you strike a bottom fish, it's no time for games. Jam the rod butt into your belly or under your arm--or best of all into a rod belt to protect your anatomy--and crank fiercely. The rod tip has to stay high. Many experienced anglers who are new to grouper fishing want to pump the rod as they do with gamefish that are inclined to run rather than hide. But this is the wrong thing to do with grouper and big snapper because each time you

128

drop the rod to gain slack, the fish gets his head down and bores back toward his hiding spot. The trick is to snatch the hook home and start reeling like mad at the same time, with the rod still as high as you can hold it.

Keep right on winching with all your might until you've gained at least 20 feet of line. If you don't, any large fish will nearly always dive into a rocky cave where you can't lever it out. Get them up that first 20 feet, though, and they're less single-minded about getting to their hidey hole--you have time to play the fish at that point.

Many experienced skippers are convinced that if you lose two or three fish from a hole, their drumming and panicked behavior will shut down all the other grouper on the reef. So use enough gun and work hard to put those early fish in the boat.

For really big grouper, 25 pounds and up, you may not be able to keep the rod up after the initial strike. Anglers who go after the giant copperbelly gags off the Florida Panhandle in water over 200 feet deep use 80-pound gear and "rail braces", which are notches to hold the rod so that it can be levered up and down to hoist the fish off bottom. It's brutal, non-IGFA-approved--and effective. Of course, if you tackle the reef giants--cubera, warsaw grouper and the like--a fighting chair and kidney harness are not out of the question.

SOLVING SNAGS

If a fish does go in a rock, you can often get it to come out by slackening the line completely and putting the rod aside for a few minutes. The fish soon forgets its fright and eases out of the rock. If you pick up the rod carefully, take up slack and then crank and pull with all your might, you can usually get it started toward the top before it can dive back to the refuge.

Another tactic is to "strum" the fish out, putting tension on the line and then plucking at it to send vibrations down to the hook. This works sporadically, but it's worth a try when nothing else will budge a stubborn fish.

HOOKING TACTICS FOR JIGS

Some smart anglers like to use a heavy rod armed with a large circle hook to put down a "monster bait", a grunt about 8 inches long. This bait is lowered almost but not quite to bottom, and the rod put in the holder while anglers use smaller live baits, jigs or cut bait on lighter gear to catch the typical potpourri. If there's a whopper grouper on the reef, sooner or later he'll swim by the grunt, grab it and hook himself on the circle hook-- it doesn't require a hook set to dig in.

According to Capt. Dave Zalewski of Clearwater, Fla., putting a large jig on bottom and setting the rod in the holder also does the job on big fish.

"Grouper are curious," says Zalewski. "That jig flutters up and down just a little with the wave action on the boat, and eventually the biggest grouper on the rock can't stand it and he'll grab hold."

In deep water, some grouper anglers are having success with "Coon Pop" jigs of the sort devised by Louisiana tarpon fishermen and recently copied by silver king anglers in Florida. Basically, you use a nylon tie wrap to fasten a 4 to 6 ounce jig head and body, with the hook cut off, to the lower bend of a 7/0 circle hook. The jig is lowered all the way to bottom, then cranked up one revolution of the spool and allowed to hang in the tide. Again, it's best to simply hang on. Circle hooks work best when they do the hook-setting on their own--just start reeling when the rod begins to bend.

Bottom line on bottom fishing: practice will give you the touch. You may make a thousand "water-hauls" before you start hooking fish consistently, but if you use good tackle and pay attention, you'll soon be one of the hot sticks aboard any boat.

16

BOATS FOR BOTTOM FISHING

Don't think about it too hard. At the cost of a suitable offshore rig, plus the required 50 to 100 gallons of fuel per trip, tackle, ice, bait and snacks, it's probable that grouper and snapper fillets are the most expensive meat in the world. But you gotta do what you gotta do, and the big bite, the boat itself, will give you and your family years of quality time together. Plus, if you buy right, you can recoup a reasonable portion of the investment when you're ready to sell.

BASIC RIGS

Boats that will let you get out to where the grouper and snapper are biting most of the year begin at about 20 feet long and a cost of about $20,000. The center console 20 to 25 feet long is the workhorse, probably responsible for far more grouper and snapper than all other boats combined. But not all 20-foot boats are created equal. Freeboard and bottom design are the main determinates. A 20-footer with only a couple feet of freeboard forward is not adequate on most days, while a boat with the same LOA and 48 inches above the water at the bow is a serious offshore boat.

Hull flare is also a factor. More flare makes it possible for a boat to nose into a wave and be raised up above it as the force of the water lifts on the ever broader surface. Flair also helps to knock down spray, providing a more comfortable ride.

And, since a bottom-fishing boat spends a lot of its time at anchor well offshore, stability at rest is a major factor. This means a boat with broad chines and somewhat less vee than the performance king mackerel tournament rigs is ideal. The flatter the bottom, the rougher the ride on the way out, but the smoother it sits when anchored. Like most things in hull design, the best rig for you depends on your personal preferences.

FAMILY RIGS

Probably the ideal family rig for grouper and medium-range pelagic fishing is a walk-around cabin boat 21 to 25 feet long. This is big enough to provide fishing space and sea-handling capabilities, small enough to be within reach economically for many anglers, and the cabin provides a spot to hide that all-important Porta-Potti. The cabin also makes a good spot to lock up rods and assorted gear, and is big enough to hold a small family for overnighting. Cockpits provide plenty of fishing space both for trolling and for live-baiting, and the walk-around makes it easy to get to the bow to raise and lower the anchor.

Most walk-arounds in this size range have 3 to 4 feet of freeboard at the bow, which makes them seaworthy, plus tall windshields that help keep the spray off everyone. Most also come equipped with a top, and you can get optional zip-on plexi-glass weather guards which convert the helm station into a comfortable place to work in any weather. For the family fisherman, these rigs are hard to beat because they provide so much more protection from wind and spray than the center console configuration. And since most everyone fishes from the stern when after bottom fish-- because that's where the transducer from the depthfinder is located and consequently the part the fish are directly under-- the added bow space in a center console usually goes to waste.

Center console rigs account for the bulk of the grouper catch out of most Florida ports. The open space at the bow is good for jiggers. Note the downriggers aft.

A V6 outboard, probably mounted on a bracket to allow for a full transom, is the usual power-choice for the walk-around. A 150 will push a 21 adequately, while a 200 is ideal. Choose a 225 for the 23- and 25-foot rigs. (Opt for the new saltwater models produced by most builders--they're designed with special corrosion protection that standard V6's lack.) You can expect fuel economy of around 2 to 2.5 mpg with these rigs run at moderate rpms.

All of these rigs will have cruising speeds in the low 30's, and max out in the middle to high 40's. Fuel consumption is likely to approach 3 mpg at the most economical speed, usually around 3500 to 4000 rpms with an outboard. This ain't fast, but it's as fast as you'll want to run in anything but flat calm offshore.

Choose a full transom with a bracket, rather than the conventional cut-out transom mounting for the outboard. You gain usable space, get a built-in swim platform as an extra, and cut the noise heard at the helm. The full transom gives you 18 inches to 2 feet more protection from waves rolling aboard over the stern, and many boats also run faster and use less fuel with the motor mounted on a bracket, because the prop gets a bite on ''cleaner'' water further aft of the transom.

If you can afford it, two motors are definitely better than one for offshore operation. In many installations, just one of the motors will put your boat on plane and bring you home at close to 30 mph. It's a great security blanket, plus the added charging system of the second motor provides insurance that you won't run down your batteries by working the chum grinder too long. On the down side, the typical V6 goes for 10 grand and up these days, and you cut your fuel mileage to about a mile per gallon when you run two instead of one.

LAYOUT AND RIGGING

For serious bottom-digger, a large, well aerated baitwell is a must--at least 35 gallons, without square corners, and powerfully charged by big raw-water pumps.

The well should be as far aft as possible, so that the bait is where you need it, at the back of the cockpit. On large boats, some designers sink it right into the full transom, which is ideal. This may put too much weight too far aft on some boats under 25 feet long, though--in these, best location may be integral with the leaning post in a center console, or perhaps behind the helm seat in a cabin rig. Floor wells are nicely hidden, and they put the bait down low where it won't get battered as the boat jumps rough seas.

When it comes to fish boxes, make sure they're well insulated. Most floor boxes will be insulated by the foam flotation pumped into the hull, but not all boats over 20 feet have this flotation. Above-decks wells are not necessarily insulated. If not, they'll

Walk-around cabin rigs are ideal for families who enjoy reef fishing. The cabin allows a private head, plus a place to get out of the weather, yet there's plenty of fishing space in the cockpit.

be serviceable for day-trips, but not good if you do entire weekends at sea.

Any boat that uses chum needs a sea-water washdown system. It's often offered in a package with a raw-water baitwell pump at moderate extra cost. Get a short length of hose to go with it so you can reach all corners of the boat to rinse away the slime before it dries.

You need plenty of rod holders, of course--four verticals for trolling, six or more horizontals under the gunnels or inside the cabin for keeping backups.

When grouper move into Boca Grande Pass in early spring, even a low-cut rig like this one is adequate for jigging up some fish fingers.

And if you have the extra change, a fiberglass hard-top is worth the extra $2500 to $3500 price tag. It provides permanent shade for the helm, which can make you feel a hundred percent stronger at the end of a hot day. The hard top also offers a good place to secure electronics out of the way except when you need them.

The top also usually comes equipped with tubes to hold a half-dozen rods out of the way and up out of the spray, and can be used as a high anchor point for your radio antenna, loran antenna and GPS module, plus outriggers.

In general, whatever boat and rigging you opt for, choose one of the well-known names in the business, one that's been around for a while and that does plenty of advertising. These may not necessarily be better than the newest hull on the block, but they have a reputation built over time, which makes it likely you'll get a dependable product--and one that you can sell without taking a total bath at resale time, as is likely to be the case if you buy an off-brand.

Buying used is a little risky with a saltwater rig, but if you find one that's been well-cared for you can save up to half the price of a new rig. Motors are the major concern, of course, but sometimes you can make hay by finding a solid hull with a smoked motor. The owner can't use it and probably can't sell it at a decent price, so you can buy it for a song and install a new motor that will give you years of service. (Just make sure it hasn't been sunk--look in the bilge for sand, and check the wiring for tell-tale green corrosion. A boat that has been to the bottom will require replacement of every metal part aboard, a bigger job than most want to tackle.)

17

FISH CARE AND COOKING

Because the reef species live far from land in clean, open water, they never disappoint on the table. Grouper, snapper and other reef fishes are the prime treats the sea offers. Their meat is white, firm and mild, and even the larger fish remain great table fare.

They're great when they come out of the water, that is. Whether they stay great depends on the treatment they receive.

THE BIG CHILL

First, any bottom-digger should own a big-league ice chest, one of the jumbos four feet long with roped-on carrying handles adequate to lift a couple hundred pounds. (Think big and you'll catch big--maybe!) A big box also holds the necessary amount of ice to cool big fish. A single bag of ice won't do for a catch of 10 or 15 fish of 10 pounds or better. The best solution is to visit an ice house on your way to the ramp and load the chest with ice chips, all the way to the top. As it melts, it makes room for the fish, and because it molds itself around the carcasses, it keeps them extremely cold.

Second choice is to lay a couple blocks of ice in the bottom of the box, and then reserve three or four bags of cubes to scatter over the fish as they're caught. The blocks won't melt for several days, and help the cubes to last longer.

With all icing systems, be sure to keep the drain plug out of the box so excess water runs off. Lying in a pool of fresh water at the bottom of the ice chest will ruin any fish. With built-in fish boxes, use only those that are above the water-line and self-bailing, or that have pump-out systems.

Incidentally, when you put fish on ice, they tend to shrink as the muscles chill. In an actual test, I once measured a fresh-caught gag at 21 inches when it came out of the water. After it had been on ice for a couple of hours, the fish taped a half-inch shorter. If you keep fish that barely make the minimum size limit and store them on ice, you may have "shorts" when the marine patrol gets out their yardstick. It's smart to allow at least an inch more than the minimum to provide for this shrinkage.

(An aside here--while fresh fish have very little odor, the slime they leave behind creates a terrible stench if not cleaned out of boxes completely. The best cleaning solutions I've found is Clorox Clean-Up with bleach, a kitchen spray cleaner. A few shots of this stuff eats away slime and dirt, kills bacteria and keeps the box looking and smelling clean. Just don't get it on your clothes or cloth upholstery--it makes white spots immediately.)

If you're going to be out more than a day, fish should be gutted shortly after they're caught. In most states reef fish have to be landed whole so that the marine patrol can measure for length if they check your catch, but there's no rule against removing the entrails, and these are what cause early deterioration of fish.

CLEANING

Naturally, all fish should be cleaned and frozen or cooked as soon as possible.

Capt. Jim Bradley of Weeki Wachee, Florida, cleans about as many big grouper as anybody on the Gulf, and he swears by electric knives. He can knock the filets off in two quick cuts and two more swipes do away with the skin. The rib cage goes next (he may save it for the chowder pot, though) and the job is done. Just be sure to use a grounded socket and wear rubber-soled shoes when you use an electric knife, because when you're standing on wet cement, there is a danger of serious electric shock if something goes wrong.

For small snapper, some anglers prefer to simply remove head, tail and entrails, scrape away the scales and fry the fish whole. This leaves bones to deal with, but keeping the skin in place makes the fish more moist and the meat less greasy.

KNIVES AND SHARPENING

Among conventional knives, Forschner makes some of the best, as does Chicago Cutlery. An 8-incher (blade measure) is adequate, with a 6-incher for fine work. If your fish run large, go for a 10-incher. And keep a steel at your side, making a couple back strokes on it after EACH FISH. (A "back stroke" is just the reverse of a sharpening stroke, but it's more important when you have a good edge to start with. The back stroke bends the fine wire edge of the knife back to align with the thicker sections of the blade, which means you can keep cutting easily for far longer. When you draw your knife backwards along the steel at the right angle, you can feel it working against the serrations in the sharpener--there's a certain amount of drag. If it slides smoothly with no drag, you don't have the angle quite right.)

RECIPES

First, a couple words on blackened grouper and snapper. Forget it.

Blackening is for fish like carp and black drum, that are, to put it delicately, as palatable as road killed possum. The peppering and carboning covers up the natural flavor of the fillet. This is the last thing you want to do to the yummy bottom species.

OK, I'll admit it, I've tried it and it's very good. But I normally reserve the blackening treatment for stuff like AJ's, bluefish, mackerel, etc. If you've just gotta try, here's a recipe:

141

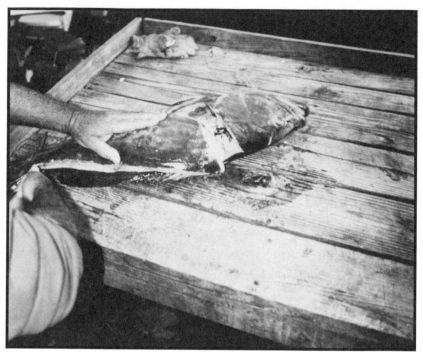

Captain Jim Bradley of Weeki Wachee, Florida, shows how to fillet a grouper with two movements of the electric knife. Grouper taste best when skinned and boned.

BLACKENED GROUPER

Blackening is another word for burning. You burn the outer layer black in a smoking hot iron skillet, preferably outside over a propane burner because it makes some soot and smoke. Dust small, boned fillets with a mix made of cayenne pepper, onion powder, garlic powder, salt, black pepper and oregano--less cayenne if you have no Cajun inclinations, more if you love the heat. Melt a half-stick of butter into a smoking hot pan, then immediately add the fillets. Stand right there with the spatula at the ready because each side cooks in a little over a minute and if you leave it too long you have charcoal instead of blackened fish. It's good, but you can't tell if it's grouper or garfish.

GROUPER FINGERS

Probably the tastiest way to cook both grouper and snapper is to cut the meat into "fingers", dip them in milk and then in seasoned flour, and deep fry in vegetable oil. This won't do much for your diet, but it's absolutely wonderful on the tongue. Drain on several layers of paper towels before serving.

GRILLED SNAPPER

Also super, and a lot less trouble, is to simply clamp the fillets in a grilling basket and toss them on the charcoal. I spread a bit of mayo on both sides to help the meat to brown, and add a little tang of lemon. Or, you can drizzle the fillets with Terriyaki sauce before and during cooking. (Tip--spray the basket with Pam or other non-stick coating, and also spray the fillets with this oil before cooking. Otherwise, the meat sticks to the basket.)

BAKED REEF

Baked grouper, scamp, mangrove or red snapper is also a delight. For the basic dish, just use the skinned, boned filets laid in an oiled cooking pan, and sprinkle a little basil and oregano over the top, plus a drizzle of liquid margarine if you're not watching the weight. Maybe add a shake of paprika for color. This is reef fish in its purest form, and the only thing you taste is the lovely, light meat itself. Bake at about 350 until the meat just flakes, before it begins to dry.

If you want something a little more complex, you can add all sorts of sauces or toppings to the fish. One easy approach is to float the meat in New England clam chowder and toss a scatter of fresh chopped onions on top. Or you can add mozzarella cheese, and finish off by broiling until the cheese just turns brown. For a strong-flavored dish, top the fillets with Mexican style stewed tomatoes, which have bits of jalapeno added, and add a very light sprinkle of chili powder to the top of each fillet.

Bottom line is there's no bad way to cook grouper, snapper and other reef species. These are fish made to be eaten.

FISH POISONING

Ciguetera is a nasty form of fish poisoning, caused by eating saltwater fish--including sometimes grouper--that have gobbled up certain types of smaller critters found on tropical coral reefs. Symptoms include tingling of the lips, tongue and throat within 24 hours of the meal. After it really sets in, the victims feel nausea and stomach cramps, usually followed by vomiting and diarrhea. The vision blurs in some cases, and the skin breaks out in a rash. In severe cases, muscular coordination breaks down and breathing becomes difficult. There have been deaths from ciguetera--it's clearly not your average nose cold. There's not much in the way of successful treatment; getting better takes months.

Fish poisoning is most common from eating large barracuda from some areas of the Caribbean--but in other areas, including Belize and along the west coast of Florida, locals consider cuda's up to 10 pounds completely safe and eat every one they catch. I've eaten the meat myself in both places and it's delicious.

Gag and red grouper have rarely been implicated in ciguetera, but yellowfins and the largest blacks, warsaws and jewfish have been. It seems likely that the poison builds up cumulatively, sort of like mercury in polluted waters, which is why the largest specimens are most likely to cause problems.

There is still not any effective way to tell if a slab of fish will cause problems. The live fish looks the same as any other fish and is completely healthy. The fillets don't look any different. And all the folk-lore advice is baloney according to doctors who deal with the stuff--meat with ciguetera does not turn a silver coin black, and dogs, cats and ants will eat it readily. (No report on whether they feel tingling around their little lips afterwards.) Best advice is to avoid the suspect species at weights over 10 pounds, and to check with locals when you go on a trip to a new locale to see whether there have been cases in the area.

18

FISH WITH THE PROS

There's no question that a few days offshore with an expert reef fisherman can improve catches on your personal trips enormously. There's no substitute for the hands-on education professional skippers can provide because their expertise is honed by spending more time on the water in a year than most of us will fish in our lifetimes.

And, most successful charterboaters are good teachers--they have to be in order to get their anglers to catch fish, and consequently to come back next year. Most are happy to share their tactics--but not their loran numbers!

For the occasional angler or those who own small boats not suitable for offshore operation, chartering a boat with a competent skipper also makes a lot of economic sense. The $350 to $600 charter cost can be split by up to six anglers, making the trips affordable for almost anyone. And all the tackle and bait is already aboard--all you have to do is show up. (You don't get stuck with washing down the boat afterward, or with buying the fuel for it, either.)

While the best catches of large fish are usually taken from charterboats, "head boats" or party boats produce lots of smaller fish on their half-day trips to well-known reefs. And some of

Guides know all the secret numbers, and also can teach you more about reef tactics in a day than you'd learn in years on your own.

these big boats specialize in overnight runs to distant reefs that are actually beyond the range of most charterboats. These trips often produce spectacular catches of monster grouper and snapper, and they provide all the comforts of home including air-conditioned restaurants and sleeping quarters. The half-day trips go for as little as $35 including tackle rental, while the overnight trips average $85 and up.

The following list includes mostly skippers who specialize in offshore work, though you'll also find some here whose expertise is inshore snapper angling. The author has not fished with all of those listed, but they're all well-known, productive anglers who can find the fish anytime they're biting.

GUIDES

Capt. Tim Adams, Orange Beach, AL (334) 981-6726
Capt. Sonny Alawine, Orange Beach, AL (334) 981-3936
Capt. Jim Bradley, Weeki Wachee, FL, (904) 596-5639
Capt. Larry Blue, St. Petersburg, FL (813) 595-4798
Capt. Nathan Cox, Orange Beach, AL (334) 981-3733
Capt. John Dudas, Miami, FL, (305) 361-9318
Capt. Dennis Forgione, North Miami, FL (305) 651-8478
Capt. Richard Howard, Clearwater Bch, FL (813) 446-8962
Capt. Ron Green, Islamorada, FL (800) 336-9093
Capt. Andy Griffiths, Jr., Key West, FL (305) 296-2639
Capt. Johnny Lee, Orange Beach, AL (334) 989-6874
Capt. George Mitchell, Miami, (305) 238-6592
Capt. Bob Fazioli, Sarasota, FL (813) 758-5953
Capt. John O'Hanlon, Clearwater, FL (813) 786-3175
Capt. Mark Houghtaling, Miami, (305) 253-1151
Capt. Joe Penovich, Port Canaveral, FL, (407) 453-3474
Capt. Jim Sharp, Big Pine Key, FL, (800) 238-1746
Capt. Bouncer Smith, Miami, FL, (305) 431-7530
Capt. J. T. Thomas, Clearwater, (813) 581-3452
Capt. Robert Trosset, Key West, FL, (305) 294-5801
Capt. Bob Walker, Orange Beach, AL (334) 981-6721
Capt. Don Walker, Orange Beach, AL (334) 981-6721
Capt. Chris Turner, St. Petersburg, FL (813) 367-1268
Capt. Dave Zalewski, Largo, FL (813) 397-8815

PARTY BOATS

Alabama Charters, Naples, FL (813) 262-3317
Double Eagle, Clearwater, FL (813) 446-1653

PARTY BOATS (cont'd.)

Florida Fisherman II, Madeira Beach, FL (800) 755-0677
Florida Fish Finder, Key West, FL (800) 878-3474
Hubbard's Sea Adventures, Madeira Bch, FL (813) 398-6577
Miss Pass-A-Grille, St. Petersburg Beach, FL (813) 360-2082
Ranger V, Treasure Island, FL (813) 391-6810
Ultimate Adventures, Naples, FL (813) 262-3080
Yankee Fleet, Key West, FL (800) 634-0939

Larsen's Outdoor Publishing
OUTDOORS/NATURE
RESOURCE DIRECTORY

If you are interested in more productive fishing, hunting and diving trips, this information is for you!

Learn how to be more successful on your next outdoor venture from these secrets, tips and tactics. Larsen's Outdoor Publishing offers informational-type books that focus on how and where to catch the most popular sport fish, hunt the most popular game or travel to productive or exciting destinations.

The perfect-bound, soft-cover books include numerous illustrative graphics, line drawings, maps and photographs. Many of our **LIBRARIES** are nationwide in scope. Others cover the Gulf and Atlantic coasts from Florida to Texas to Maryland and some foreign waters. One **SERIES** focuses on the top lakes, rivers and creeks in the nation's most visited largemouth bass fishing state.

All series appeal to outdoors readers of all skill levels. Their unique four-color cover design, interior layout, quality, information content and economical price makes these books your best source of knowledge. **Best of all, you will know how to be more successful in your outdoor endeavors!!**

BASS SERIES LIBRARY
by Larry Larsen

(BSL1) FOLLOW THE FORAGE - BASS/PREY RELATIONSHIP - Learn how to determine dominant forage in a body of water and catch more bass!

(BSL2) VOL. 2 BETTER BASS ANGLING TECHNIQUES - Learn why one lure or bait is more successful than others and how to use each lure under varying conditions.

(BSL3) BASS PRO STRATEGIES - Professional fishermen know how changes in pH, water level, temperature and color affect bass fishing, and they know how to adapt to weather and topographical variations. Learn from their experience.

(BSL4) BASS LURES - TRICKS & TECHNIQUES - When bass become accustomed to the same artificials and presentations seen over and over again, they become harder to catch. You will learn how to modify your lures and rigs and how to develop new presentation and retrieve methods to spark the interest of largemouth!

(BSL5) SHALLOW WATER BASS - Bass spend 90% of their time in waters less than 15 feet deep. Learn productive new tactics that you can apply in marshes, estuaries, reservoirs, lakes, creeks and small ponds, and you'll triple your results!

> ### HAVE THEM ALL!
> *"Larry, I'm ordering one book to give a friend for his birthday and your two new ones. I have all the BASS SERIES LIBRARY except one, otherwise I would have ordered an autographed set. I have followed your writings for years and consider them the best of the best!"*
> J. Vinson, Cataula, GA

(BSL6) BASS FISHING FACTS - Learn why and how bass behave during pre- and post-spawn, how they utilize their senses when active and how they respond to their environment, and you'll increase your bass angling success!

(BSL7) TROPHY BASS - If you're more interested in wrestling with one or two monster largemouth than with a "panful" of yearlings, then learn what techniques and locations will improve your chances.

(BSL8) ANGLER'S GUIDE TO BASS PATTERNS - Catch bass every time out by learning how to develop a productive pattern quickly and effectively. "Bass Patterns" is a reference source for all anglers, regardless of where they live or their skill level. Learn how to choose the right lure, presentation and habitat under various weather and environmental conditions!

> ### TWO TROPHIES!
> *"By using your techniques and reading your Bass Series Library of books, I was able to catch the two biggest bass I've ever caught!"*
> B. Conley, Cromwell, IN

(BSL9) BASS GUIDE TIPS - Learn secret techniques known only in a certain region or state that often work in waters all around the country. It's this new approach that usually results in excellent bass angling success. Learn how to apply what the country's top guides know!

Nine Great Volumes To Help You Catch More and Larger Bass!

(LB1) LARRY LARSEN ON BASS TACTICS

is the ultimate "how-to" book that focuses on proven productive methods. **Hundreds of highlighted tips and drawings in our LARSEN ON BASS SERIES explain how you can catch more and larger bass in waters all around the country.** This reference source by America's best known bass fishing writer will be invaluable to both the avid novice and expert angler!

(V1) VIDEO -ADVANCED BASS FISHING TACTICS

with Larry Larsen This 50-minute video is dedicated to serious anglers - those who are truly interested in learning more about the sport and in catching more and larger bass each trip. Part I details how to catch more bass from aquatic vegetaion; Part II covers tips to most effectively fish docks & piers; Part III involves trolling strategies for bigger fish, and Part IV outlines using electronics to locate bass in deep waters.

(PF1) PEACOCK BASS EXPLOSIONS! by Larry Larsen

A must read for those anglers who are interested in catching the world's most exciting fresh water fish! Detailed tips, trip planning and tactics for peacocks in South Florida, Venezuela, Brazil, Puerto Rico, Hawaii and other destinations. This book explores the most effective tactics to take the aggressive peacock bass. Invaluable to all adventurous anglers!

(PF2) PEACOCK BASS & OTHER FIERCE EXOTICS by Larry Larsen

Book 2 in the Series reveals the latest techniques and best spots to prepare you for the greatest fishing experience of your life! You'll learn how to catch more and larger fish using the valuable information from the author and expert angler, a four-time peacock bass world-record holder. It's the first comprehensive discussion on this wild and colorful fish. With stops in Peru, Colombia, Venezuela and Brazil, he provides information about colorful monster payara, and other exotic fish.

BASS WATERS GUIDE SERIES by Larry Larsen

The most productive bass waters are described in this multi-volume series, including ramps, seasonal tactics, water characteristics, etc. Many maps and photos detail specific locations.

(BW1) GUIDE TO NORTH FLORIDA BASS WATERS - Covers from Orange Lake north and west. Includes Lakes Lochloosa, Talquin and Seminole, the St. Johns, Nassau, Suwannee and Apalachicola Rivers; Newnans Lake, St. Mary's River, Juniper Lake, Ortega River, Lake Jackson, Deer Point Lake, Panhandle Mill Ponds and many more!

(BW2) GUIDE TO CENTRAL FLORIDA BASS WATERS - Covers from Tampa/ Orlando to Palatka. Includes Lakes George, Rodman, Monroe, Tarpon and the Harris Chain, the St. Johns, Oklawaha and Withlacoochee Rivers, the Ocala Forest, Crystal River, Hillsborough River, Conway Chain, Homosassa River, Lake Minneola, Lake Weir, Lake Hart, Spring Runs and many more!

(BW3) GUIDE TO SOUTH FLORIDA BASS WATERS - Covers from I-4 to the Everglades. Includes Lakes Tohopekaliga, Kissimmee, Okeechobee, Poinsett, Tenoroc and Blue Cypress, the Winter Haven Chain, Fellsmere Farm 13. Caloosahatchee River, Lake June-in-Winter, the Everglades, Lake Istokpoga, Peace River, Crooked Lake, Lake Osborne, St. Lucie Canal, Shell Creek, Lake Marian, Lake Pierce, Webb Lake and many more!

OUTDOOR TRAVEL SERIES
by Larry Larsen and M. Timothy O'Keefe

Candid guides on the best charters, time of the year, and other recommendations that can make your next fishing and/or diving trip much more enjoyable.

(OT1) FISH & DIVE THE CARIBBEAN - Vol. 1 Northern Caribbean, including Cozumel, Cayman Islands, Bahamas, Jamaica, Virgin Islands. Required reading for fishing and diving enthusiasts who want to know the most cost-effective means to enjoy these and other Caribbean islands.

(OT3) FISH & DIVE FLORIDA & The Keys - Where and how to plan a vacation to America's most popular fishing and diving destination. Features include artificial reef loran numbers; freshwater springs/caves; coral reefs/barrier islands; gulf stream/passes; inshore flats/channels; and back country estuaries.

> **BEST BOOK CONTENT!**
> *"Fish & Dive the Caribbean" was a finalist in the Best Book Content Category of the National Association of Independent Publishers (NAIP). Over 500 books were submitted by publishers including Simon & Schuster and Turner Publishing. Said the judges "An excellent source book with invaluable instructions. Written by two nationally-known experts who, indeed, know what vacationing can be!"*

DIVING / NATURE SERIES by M. Timothy O'Keefe

(DL1) DIVING TO ADVENTURE shows how to get started in underwater photography, how to use current to your advantage, how to avoid seasickness, how to dive safely after dark, and how to plan a dive vacation, including live-aboard diving.

(DL2) MANATEES - OUR VANISHING MERMAIDS is an in-depth overview of nature's strangest-looking, gentlest animals. They're among America's most endangered mammals. The book covers where to see manatees while diving, why they may be living fossils, their unique life cycle, and much more.

(DL3) SEA TURTLES - THE WATCHERS' GUIDE - Discover how and where you can witness sea turtles nesting in Florida. This book not only gives an excellent overview of sea turtle life, it also provides the specifics of appropriate personal conduct and behavior for human beings on turtle nesting beaches.

(OC1) UNCLE HOMER'S OUTDOOR CHUCKLE BOOK by Homer Circle, Fishing Editor, Sports Afield In his inimitable humorous style, "Uncle Homer" relates jokes, tales, personal anecdotes and experiences covering several decades in the outdoors.

OUTDOOR ADVENTURE by Vin T. Sparano, Outdoor Life

(OA1) HUNTING DANGEROUS GAME - Live the adventure of hunting those dangerous animals that hunt back! Track a rogue elephant, survive a grizzly attack, and face a charging Cape buffalo. These classic tales will make you very nervous next time you're in the woods!

> **KEEP ME UPDATED!**
> *"I would like to get on your mailing list. I really enjoy your books!"*
> G. Granger, Cypress, CA

(OA2) GAME BIRDS & GUN 'DOGS - A unique collection of tales about hunters, their dogs and the upland game and waterfowl they hunt. You will read about good gun dogs and heart-breaking dogs, but never about bad dogs, because there's no such animal.

COASTAL FISHING GUIDES
by Frank Sargeant

A unique "where-to" series of detailed secret spots for Florida's finest saltwater fishing. These guide books describe hundreds of little-known honeyholes and exactly how to fish them. Prime seasons, baits and lures, marinas and dozens of detailed maps of the prime spots are included. The comprehensive index helps the reader to further pinpoint productive areas and tactics. Over $160 worth of personally-marked NOAA charts in the two books.

(FG1) FRANK SARGEANT'S SECRET SPOTS Tampa Bay to Cedar Key Covers Hillsborough River and Davis Island through the Manatee River, Mullet Key and the Suwannee River.

(FG2) FRANK SARGEANT'S SECRET SPOTS Southwest Florida Covers from Sarasota Bay to Marco.

INSHORE SERIES by Frank Sargeant

(IL1) THE SNOOK BOOK-Every aspect of how you can find and catch big snook is covered, in all seasons and all waters where snook are found.

(IL2) THE REDFISH BOOK-Packed with every aspect of finding and fooling giant reds. You'll learn secret techniques revealed for the first time. After reading this informative book, you'll catch more redfish on your next trip!

(IL3) THE TARPON BOOK-Find and catch the wily "silver king" along the Gulf Coast, north through the mid-Atlantic, and south along Central and South American coastlines.

(IL4) THE TROUT BOOK -Jammed with tips for both the old salt and the rank amateur who pursue the spotted weakfish, or seatrout, throughout the coastal waters of the Gulf and Atlantic.

SALTWATER SERIES
by Frank Sargeant

(SW1) THE REEF FISHING BOOK - An all-in-one compilation of the best techniques, lures and locations for grouper and snapper and other reef species, including how to find and catch live bait, trolling techniques and the latest rod and reels for success. Learn the secrets of top charterboat professionals for finding and catching big grouper and snapper year around, throughout the 2,000-mile coastal range of these much-sought fish! Special features include where the biggest fish live, electronics savvy, anchoring tricks and much more!

HUNTING LIBRARY
by John E. Phillips

(DH1) MASTERS' SECRETS OF DEER HUNTING - Increase your deer hunting success by learning from the masters of the sport. New information on tactics and strategies is included in this book, the most comprehensive of its kind.

(DH2) THE SCIENCE OF DEER HUNTING Covers why, where and when a deer moves and deer behavior. Find the answers to many of the toughest deer hunting problems a sportsman ever encounters!

(DH3) MASTERS' SECRETS OF BOW-HUNTING DEER - Learn the skills required to take more bucks with a bow, even during gun season. A must read for those who walk into the woods with a strong bow and a swift shaft.

(DH4) HOW TO TAKE MONSTER BUCKS - Specific techniques that will almost guarantee a trophy buck next season! Includes tactics by some of the nation's most accomplished trophy buck hunters.

> ### RECOMMENDATION!
> *"Masters' Secrets of Turkey Hunting is one of the best books around. If you're looking for a good turkey book, buy it!"*
> J. Spencer, Stuttgart Daily Leader, AR
>
> ### NO BRAGGIN'!
> *"From anyone else Masters' Secrets of Deer Hunting would be bragging and unbelievable. But not with John Phillips, he's paid his dues!"* F. Snare, Brookville Star, OH

(TH1) MASTERS' SECRETS OF TURKEY HUNTING - Masters of the sport have solved some of the most difficult problems you can encounter while hunting wily longbeards with bows, blackpowder guns and shotguns. Learn the 10 deadly sins of turkey hunting.

(BP1) BLACKPOWDER HUNTING SECRETS - Learn how to take more game during and after the season with black powder guns. If you've been hunting with black powder for years, this book will teach you better tactics to use throughout the year.

FISHING LIBRARY

(CF1) MASTERS' SECRETS OF CRAPPIE FISHING by John E. Phillips Learn how to make crappie start biting again once they have stopped, select the best jig color, find crappie in a cold front, through the ice, or in 100-degree heat. Unusual, productive crappie fishing techniques are included.

(CF2) CRAPPIE TACTICS by Larry Larsen - This book will improve your catch! The book includes some basics for fun fishing, advanced techniques for year 'round crappie and tournament preparation.

> ### CRAPPIE COUP!
> *"After reading your crappie book, I'm ready to overthrow the 'crappie king' at my lakeside housing development!"*
> R. Knorr, Haines City, FL

(CF3) MASTERS' SECRETS OF CATFISHING by John E. Phillips is your best guide to catching the best-tasting, elusive cats. Learn the best time of the year, the most productive places and which states to fish in your pursuit of Mr. Whiskers.

LARSEN'S OUTDOOR PUBLISHING
CONVENIENT ORDER FORM
ALL PRICES INCLUDE POSTAGE/HANDLING

FRESH WATER
___BSL1. Better Bass Angling Vol 1 ($12.45)
___BSL2. Better Bass Angling Vol 2 ($12.45)
___BSL3. Bass Pro Strategies ($12.45)
___BSL4. Bass Lures/Techniques ($12.45)
___BSL5. Shallow Water Bass ($12.45)
___BSL6. Bass Fishing Facts ($12.45)
___BSL7. Trophy Bass ($12.45)
___BSL8. Bass Patterns ($12.45)
___BSL9. Bass Guide Tips ($12.45)
___CF1. Mstrs' Scrts/Crappie Fshng ($12.45)
___CF2. Crappie Tactics ($12.45)
___CF3. Mstr's Secrets of Catfishing ($12.45)
___LB1. Larsen on Bass Tactics ($15.45)
___PF1. Peacock Bass Explosions! ($15.95)
___PF2. Peacock Bass & Other Fierce
Exotics ($16.45)

SALT WATER
___IL1. The Snook Book ($12.45)
___IL2. The Redfish Book ($12.45)
___IL3. The Tarpon Book ($12.45)
___IL4. The Trout Book ($12.45)
___SW1. The Reef Fishing Book ($16.45)

OTHER OUTDOORS BOOKS
___DL1. Diving to Adventure ($12.45)
___DL2. Manatees/Vanishing ($11.45)
___DL3. Sea Turtles/Watchers' ($11.45)
___OC1. Outdoor Chuckle Book ($9.95)

BIG MULTI-BOOK DISCOUNT!
2-3 books, SAVE 10%
4 or more books, SAVE20%

REGIONAL
___FG1. Secret Spots-Tampa Bay/
Cedar Key   ($15.45)
___FG2. Secret Spots - SW Florida ($15.45)
___BW1. Guide/North Fl. Waters ($14.95)
___BW2. Guide/Cntral Fl.Waters ($14.95)
___BW3. Guide/South Fl.Waters ($14.95)
___OT1. Fish/Dive - Caribbean ($11.95)
___OT3. Fish/Dive Florida/ Keys ($13.95)

HUNTING
___DH1. Mstrs' Secrets/ Deer Hunting ($12.45)
___DH2. Science of Deer Hunting ($12.45)
___DH3. Mstrs' Secrets/Bowhunting ($12.45)
___DH4. How to Take Monster Bucks ($13.95)
___TH1. Mstrs' Secrets/ Turkey Hunting ($12.45)
___OA1. Hunting Dangerous Game! ($9.95)
___OA2. Game Birds & Gun Dogs ($9.95)
___BP1. Blackpowder Hunting Secrets ($14.45)

VIDEO &
SPECIAL DISCOUNT PACKAGES
___V1 - Video - Advanced Bass Tactics $29.95
___BSL - Bass Series Library (9 vol. set) $84.45
___IL - Inshore Library (4 vol. set) $37.95
___BW - Guides to Bass Waters (3 vols.) $37.95
Volume sets are autographed by each author.

INTERNATIONAL ORDERS
Send check in U.S. funds; add $4
more per book for airmail rate

ALL PRICES INCLUDE POSTAGE/HANDLING

No. of books _____ *x $*_____ *ea = $*_____   *Special Package* _____ *@ $*_____
No. of books _____ *x $*_____ *ea = $*_____   *Video (50-min) $29.95 = $*_____
*Multi-book Discount (%) $*_____   *(Pkgs include discount)= N/A*
*SUBTOTAL 1 $*_____   *SUBTOTAL 2 $*_____

_____**For Priority Mail (add $2 more per book)** $_____
TOTAL   ENCLOSED   (check or money order) $_____

*NAME*_____*ADDRESS*_____

*CITY*_____*STATE*_____*ZIP*_____

Send check or Money Order to: Larsen's Outdoor Publishing, Dept. RD96
2640 Elizabeth Place, Lakeland, FL 33813 (941)644-3381
(Sorry, no credit card orders)

INDEX

T

tackle maintenance   27
Tampa Bay   40
10,000 Islands   41
Texas   61
"The Elbow"   84
The Steeples   42
Threadfins   118
tin squids   62
trolling   55, 107
tubular glass rods   16

V

Venice   40
vertical drop   33
VHF radio   99
Virginia Beach   89

W

warsaw grouper   12, 83
waterproof charts   108
Weeki Wachee   39
white grunt   92
wire line   24

Y

yellowfins   88
yellowmouth grouper   92
yellowtail snapper   22, 77, 78